D

# The Pen

## A Collection of Today's Best Youth Writing

Edited by
Dallas Woodburn

iUniverse, Inc.
New York   Bloomington

**Dancing With The Pen**
**A Collection of Today's Best Youth Writing**

*iUniverse books may be ordered through booksellers or by contacting:*

*iUniverse
1663 Liberty Drive
Bloomington, IN 47403
www.iuniverse.com
1-800-Authors (1-800-288-4677)*

*ISBN: 978-1-4502-5459-5 (sc)
ISBN: 978-1-4502-5462-5 (ebk)*

*Printed in the United States of America*

*iUniverse rev. date: 1/26/2011*

This book is dedicated to all the young people
– and the young-at-heart – who dare to dream
beautiful dreams and who, as Winston Churchill
so wonderfully put it, *never, never, never, never give
up.*

In memory of Sandy Roberts. Journalist Bennett
Cerf said, "A person who can bring the spirit of
laughter into a room is indeed blessed." Sir Sandy,
you were a blessing to everyone who had the good
fortune of being in a room with you.

# Contents

# Special Thanks

*"The giving of love is an education in itself."*

– Eleanor Roosevelt

My special gratitude goes to Dr. Verna B. Dauterive who has spent her adult life giving love, giving education, and giving a love of education. Indeed, Dr. Dauterive is a hero for education and young people everywhere.

I was blessed to meet Dr. Dauterive last year at a University of Southern California Alumni Association dinner. More wonderfully, I had the happy fortune to be seated next her and by evening's end I felt her love, felt her passion, and felt I had a new role model in my quest to reach out and help young writers.

Dr. Dauterive is indeed a role model we can all look up to and be inspired by. She has dedicated much of her life to education – both teaching and learning – as evidenced by her 62-year career with the Los Angeles Unified School District. Here is how dedicated she was to her own education: while working for the LAUSD, she took classes at night and on weekends to earn her Master's and Doctoral degrees in Education at USC. She went on to wear many educational hats until her retirement in 2005, from serving as principal, to coordinating integration programs during the 1960s and 1970s, to a leadership role in teacher selection and recruitment. Furthermore, this remarkable woman also served on the California Commission on the Status of Women and the California Commission on Teacher Credentialing – on appointment by governors Deukmejian and Wilson, respectively – serving two terms as elected chair of each body. Her contributions, both in leadership and financial support, to USC over the past half-century are beyond numerous and beyond generous.

While her accomplishments are many and lofty, I think it speaks volumes about Dr. Dauterive that she has so graciously and enthusiastically embraced this *Dancing With The Pen* project. In a recent phone conversation, she said in her warm, friendly voice: "Dallas, I am happy and proud to help because you and I share the same passion for young people and education."

So, once again, thank you Dr. Dauterive. Your giving of love and education makes my heart dance.

# Acknowledgments

A huge thank you to iUniverse, Inc. for its generosity in supporting the publication of this book. Special thanks to Nick Thompson, Laurie Sparks, and Rachel Moore at iUniverse for the expertise, care and attention they gave this project from the get-go.

Thanks to Glamour Magazine, Sally Hansen, and Ashoka Youth Venture, whose generous grants played a crucial role in the fruition of this project.

Continued thanks to Professors Patrick Henry and Tom Knapp and the rest of my "family" at the University of Southern California Greif Center for Entrepreneurial Studies, who were there when this book was a far-off dream. They helped give my idea both the roots of a solid foundation and the wings of self-belief. I hope this book makes them proud.

Many thanks to my mentors and friends of Write On! For Literacy for their valuable advice and continual support. Though too numerous to name them all, here is a short list: Andrea Spence Accinelli,

Aimee Bender, Charles and Angela Bocage, Cynthia Brian, The Bryan Family, Jack Collins, Nanci Cone, Verna Dauterive, Jim Duran, Debra Eckerling, Larry Emrich, Susan Goodkin, B. Lynn Goodwin, Carolyn Howard-Johnson, Jeanne Finestone, Richard Fliegel, Patricia Fry, Don and Lynn Jensen, Christina Katz, Rajiv Khanna, Barry Kibrick, Ken and Kathy McAlpine, Linda McCoy-Murray, Margaret McSweeney, Erica Miner, Rima Muna, Patti and Tom Post, Deborah Reber, Ric Ruffinelli, Joe and Mari Spirito, Alicia Stratton, Tania Sussman, Shane Toogood, Bunny Vreeland, Lee Wade, Jennifer Wilkov.

Thank you also to the media outlets that have shown phenomenal support for Write On! Books before *Dancing With The Pen* was even launched: Attribute Magazine, Smart Poodle Publishing, The Reading Tub, The Ventura Breeze, and The Ventura County Star newspaper.

And, of course, thank you to the schools, teachers and staff who embraced this project with enthusiasm and aplomb. Again, there are too many to name each, but here are a key few: Kate Larsen and Cabrillo Middle School; Gina Gutierrez and CAPE Charter School; CeCe Johnson and DeAnza Middle School; Heather Drucker and Rose Avenue School; Chad Stolly and Sidney Middle School.

My deepest thanks and love to my extended family, and most especially to my parents for believing in me and reminding me of my P.A.S.T.

Finally, gratitude, pride and love to my younger-but-taller brother Greg for letting me use his beautiful artwork for this book's cover. As always, thanks to Greg (who I now look up to both literally and figuratively) for being my role model, biggest fan and best friend.

*Dancing in all its forms cannot be excluded from the curriculum of all noble education; dancing with the feet, with ideas, with words, and need I add that one must also be able to dance with the pen?*

**– Friedrich Nietzsche**

# Greetings From Dallas Woodburn

"The best children's book writers are not people who have kids, but people who write from the child within themselves."

— Andrea Brown

I would dare take Andrea Brown's wonderful thought a step further by saying: *The best children's book writers are children themselves.*

The foundation of Write On! Books – and the reason this anthology you are reading came into being – is the belief that young people need and deserve a vehicle to share their unique voices with each other, and with society as a whole. When I visit schools to speak about my own personal writing journey, I always ask the students if any of them are interested in writing. Usually a few tentative hands raise. In contrast, at the end of my talks when I ask the same question, nearly all the students excitedly thrust up their hands as if trying to touch the ceiling. Many young people tell me they didn't know kids *could* be writers.

Not only *can* kids be writers, they can be *brilliant* writers! They can write imaginative, touching, thought-provoking pieces, as this book attests. And writing, especially for young people, can create many amazing opportunities. The mission of Write On! For Literacy, which I founded in 2001, is to encourage kids to discover joy, confidence, a means of self-expression and connection to others through writing and reading. Activities and projects include writing contests, fun creative writing workshops, and an annual Holiday Book Drive that has collected and distributed more than 11,000 new books to disadvantaged kids. Visit www.writeonbooks.org for more information.

In August 2010, I entered the Master of Fine Arts (M.F.A.) Program at Purdue University to pursue my degree in Fiction Writing. What a thrilling opportunity! I will spend three years living in a supportive community of writers, writing up a storm and receiving valuable feedback on my work from professors, visiting authors and fellow students I admire. I have no doubt I will grow tremendously, as a writer and as a person, during my time in West Lafayette, Indiana.

My dream career is to write novels, continue to grow Write On! For Literacy and Write On! Books, and also teach creative writing at the university level. A Master's degree is a crucial step closer to becoming a professor. M.F.A. Programs are fiercely competitive; in many ways, being accepted to Purdue's elite program is my "big break" as a writer.

The thing about "big breaks," however, is that there are innumerable other "big breaks" that lead up to that pivotal "yes" – and, with luck and hard work, there will be more "big breaks" to follow. The old adage is true: "The journey of a thousand miles begins with a single step." Of course, you must follow that first step with a second, third, fourth step, and so on.

Here is a look back, in reverse chronological order, at the many steps that have led to my "big breaks" to date:

During the M.F.A. application process, I received excellent advice from the Creative Writing professors I studied with as an undergraduate at the University of Southern California. In particular, while at USC I was fortunate to take Fiction Writing classes with the remarkable Aimee Bender, who has become a dear mentor and friend. Aimee inspired me to tackle difficult subjects and explore new terrain in my fiction. My writing – and my self-confidence – developed in wonderful ways thanks in no small part to her steady guidance and unwavering support. In fact, one of the short stories I wrote while in her class was later nominated for a Pushcart Prize, and two others have since been published in literary journals.

If not for the growth I experienced in Aimee's class, I doubt my portfolio would have been strong enough to be accepted into Purdue's M.F.A. Program. My application was further strengthened by "big breaks" I received during my undergraduate studies: I completed my first novel manuscript, signed with the amazing literary agency Foundry Literary + Media to represent it, and experienced the revision process on a whole new level under the deft and enthusiastic guidance of my agents Yfat Reiss Gendell and Kendra Jenkins. I also served as Coordinator of the Young Writers Program of the Santa Barbara Writers Conference, published essays in the Los Angeles Times, and felt my entire view of the world expand thanks to a semester studying abroad in the seaside town of Norwich, England.

But back to Aimee for a moment, because if not for her, my entire undergraduate experience would have been vastly different. Long before I had Aimee as a professor, I was a big fan of her work, particularly her first short story collection *The Girl in the Flammable Skirt*, which coincidentally came out the same year my first self-published book, *There's a Huge Pimple On My Nose*, was released. (More on my debut book later.) Aimee was the reason I knew USC had an undergraduate Creative Writing program – and a fantastic one at that. It was a dream opportunity for an aspiring young writer. However, the cost of a private institution like USC was beyond my family's financial means. I knew if I wanted to go to USC, I needed to earn my own way through scholarships.

USC has a second-to-none merit scholarship program, and I was palms-sweating, stomach-clenching nervous during my interview for the full-tuition Trustee scholarship – especially when the interviewer asked an off-the-wall hypothetical question I had not prepared for in the least.

But instead of being flustered, instead of focusing on the pressure and high stakes, I took a deep breath and tried to remain confident in my abilities and quick-thinking skills. After all, I reminded myself, I had been in this situation before. Since publishing my first book in fifth grade and my second book in high school, I had been interviewed for dozens of radio programs and countless magazine and newspaper pieces. I had even appeared on Barry Kibrick's fabulous PBS book talk show "Between the Lines" to discuss my second collection of short stories, *3 a.m.* But the interview I recalled was one that had happened mere weeks before my USC interview: "The Early Show" on CBS. The producers flew me out from California to New York City to appear on the popular morning show, where Hannah Storm interviewed me – on live national television – about teen/parent relationships. Beforehand, the producers sent dozens of questions I might be asked and I spent weeks preparing. I was nervous, of course, but I felt confident and ready.

Then came the morning of the interview. I clearly remember sitting on the couch across from Hannah Storm, watching in panic as the cameras cut to a video clip I had not been shown or told about. The video clip featured a father and his teenage son arguing over Internet use and privacy issues. This was indeed an unexpected curveball! I had not prepared any responses or anecdotes about this topic. The butterflies in my stomach burst into frenzied flight.

Hannah turned to me for a response, and ...

... I gave her one. A coherent, authentic answer from a teen's perspective. Hannah nodded and smiled. The interview proceeded smoothly. In the Green Room afterwards, everyone told me I had been a "natural" on camera and hadn't seemed nervous at all.

So, when faced with that surprise question during my USC scholarship interview, I had self-confidence to draw upon. *At least this isn't live on national television,* I remember thinking. Then I smiled, relaxed, and answered the question.

I received the scholarship and was able to go to USC to study Creative Writing.

More "big breaks." I never would have been interviewed on "The Early Show" if not for a bi-monthly column I was writing at the time for Family Circle magazine called "What Your Teen Wants You To Know." My column tackled common teen/parent issues – chores, curfew, academic pressure, dating, financial responsibility – from a teen's perspective, the hope being that after reading my column parents would better understand where their teenagers were coming from and would be able to forge a stronger, healthier, more open and honest bond. The column began as a single article; it was so well-received that the editors asked me to expand it into a series.

To be sure, getting my article accepted by Family Circle was a long shot. I knew when I sent an e-mail to the editor pitching the idea that the odds of rejection were very high. Still, I thought, *What do I have to lose? Why not try?* I had published articles in other magazines, although admittedly none as major as Family Circle. Often when I sent queries to editors, they were dismissive, saying I was "too young" to be a writer. However, I persisted in viewing my young age not as a disadvantage, but as an *advantage*. I knew what it was like to be a teenager in the 21$^{st}$ Century. Indeed, my first published articles were in teen magazines, chronicling my high school experiences: going to Prom with a friend, getting a summer job, breaking up with my first boyfriend. My pitch to Family Circle would not have been unique or compelling if not for the fact that I was a teenager myself!

My first book began with a similar thought, tying back to the earlier quote by Andrea Brown: *Who better knows what kids want to read than a kid herself?* When I was in fifth grade, I applied for and received a $50 grant from my elementary school to do something creative. I put together a collection of stories and poems I had written, drew some illustrations, and took the manuscript to a local Kinko's copy shop, where my $50 grant allowed me to print up twenty-five staple-bound copies. My idea was to sell the book at my school and use the proceeds to repay the grant I had received so an extra grant could be offered the following year.

It was incredible to open that box of books and see my name on the cover. I swear J.K. Rowling was not more proud of her first *Harry Potter* edition! Even more incredible was bringing my books to school and selling every single copy within two days – and then being asked if I had more copies available. So I went back to Kinko's and ordered twenty-five more copies, which soon sold out as well. I eventually went to a professional print shop and ordered a large batch of glue-bound, glossy-covered copies of *There's a Huge Pimple On My Nose*.

Another "big break" was when the teachers at my elementary school asked me to speak to their classes about how I published my book. Naturally shy and more comfortable expressing myself with pen and paper, I was hesitant at first to speak in front of a group. Thankfully, the teachers were so encouraging that I swallowed my nerves and said yes. The students' response was so positive that I was asked to speak to other classes throughout the school district. I am very grateful for those teachers' support – not only did they bolster my confidence in my writing, they also nurtured my self-confidence in my speaking abilities. Now, in addition to writing, I find great joy in public speaking. Over the years, I have spoken at numerous events including the Jack London Writers Camp, the Cal Lutheran Authors Faire, and the Santa Barbara Book Festival, in addition to more than a hundred schools, youth groups, and community organizations.

Again, seeing my young age as an advantage, I sent copies of *Pimple* to newspapers and magazines in an attempt to drum up some publicity. Against long odds, it worked! *Pimple* was written about in Girls' Life and CosmoGIRL! magazines and even received a glowing review in the Los Angeles Times: "If you simply want to enjoy some remarkable writing, it would be hard to find a book more satisfying." To date, *Pimple* has sold more than 2,600 copies all across the United States.

As a result of my first ventures into book publishing, I realized that not only do I love writing, I also love sharing my writing with others. I was amazed at the power of words to forge connections across distance, culture, age, and family background. I originally thought my book would only speak to other kids in my hometown, but I soon discovered that teenagers and parents from all different places loved it as well.

However, *There's a Huge Pimple On My Nose* was not the beginning of my writing career.

My very first "big break" – what all my other writing breaks can be traced back to, from "The Early Show" to the scholarship to attend USC, from signing with Foundry Literary + Media to now entering the M.F.A. Program at Purdue – was a section called "Kids Corner" that ran every Wednesday on the back page of The Ventura County Star, my local newspaper. Every week, a writing prompt was given and kids were encouraged to send in their responses to the paper. The next week, three or four responses were published and a new prompt was given.

One week, the prompt was to write about lunchtime at school. I wrote and sent in a poem about a girl who runs out of grape jelly:

### Peanut Butter Surprise

*When I was packing my lunch one day,*
*I discovered to my dismay,*

*That we were out of grape jelly!*
*What else could I use to fill my belly?*

*A peanut butter and lettuce sandwich? No way!*
*A peanut butter and mayonnaise sandwich? Not today!*

*How about peanut butter and jellyfish?*
*Now that sounds like quite a dish.*

*So I plopped it on a piece of bread.*
*"What am I thinking?" to myself I said.*

*I tried to sell it to my friend for a buck.*
*She said no. I ate it. Yuck!*

Each Wednesday, I would eagerly turn to the back page and scan the "Kids Corner" responses to see if my entry had been chosen. I vividly remember the morning I saw my name and my words on that newsprint page for all the world (or, at least, some of my hometown) to see. I felt proud and energized – the excitement of Christmas morning paled in comparison. My self-confidence blossomed. My love of writing intensified. I wanted to be a writer. I now *saw* myself as a writer!

For many of the young writers featured in the coming pages, this anthology is the first time they will see their words and by-lines in print. I hope they feel the same rush of excitement and pride I felt upon seeing "Peanut Butter Surprise."

To our talented contributors in these pages: I hope this book brings you renewed joy, deep pride, and lasting confidence. I hope you autograph copies for your friends and family. I hope you feel part of a remarkable and ever-growing community of gifted young writers. And I hope you take this "big break" and run with it. I am confident it will be just one of many "big breaks" for each of you. Never doubt the amazing things you can accomplish. Carry this experience inside you and turn back to it if ever you feel discouraged. Most of all, always remember this: your ideas and heart and voice are valued. No one else sees the world in exactly the same way you do. Only *you* can tell your story.

Thank you for having the courage to pick up a pen and dance.

# Lightning Strikes

## by Emily Amaro

The lightning strikes the moonlit ground –
BOOM!
There's the thunder.
Everything is waiting,
until –
CRACKLE,
SNAP,
POP!
The lightning flashes.
We sit and watch
and then all is still.
It's over.

*Emily Amaro currently lives in Buckner, Missouri with her mom, dad, sister and two dogs. She enjoys writing (poetry mostly) and playing with her dogs. She would love to have another poem published in the future.*

# The Wolf's Defense: A Speech To Defend The Big Bad Wolf In Court

*by Zoe Appleby*

"We gather here today in this courtroom to discuss this Wolf's crimes. But first I ask, are they truly crimes? How would you feel if you were in the Big Bad Wolf's place?

"Please, think reasonably: is it not utterly foolish – no, completely stupid – to build houses out of straw or sticks? Such flimsy houses could not stand for very long in rain, much less in fierce wind. I would argue that the first two pigs could not have survived long in such hastily built houses. In a way, you could say the Wolf taught the pigs an important lesson about workmanship.

"Now we come to the Wolf. I would hypothesize that there was not sufficient food in the forest where he lived. Why else would he come out of the forest? The forest is his protection, his home.

"Let me ask you this: if you were starving, would you not eat just about any food you could find?

"Moreover, if you saw your favorite food in an open plastic bag on your table, would you not try to eat it? If you knew that three helpings of your favorite food were in a sealed tin can, would you not try to get the food? This is how I think the Wolf felt.

"Also, I want to point out that we never hear anything about the Wolf's family or friends, or even that any other wolves exist in this forest. We only hear about the Big Bad Wolf. Well, I say that being the only wolf in the forest would get pretty lonely. It is indeed possible the Wolf went crazy with loneliness. Being somewhat crazy and very hungry may have caused the Wolf to do what he did.

"In closing, I beg of you, do not punish this innocent Wolf for what you may call a crime, but I call an act of survival."

*Zoe Appleby is an eighth-grader attending Isbell Middle School in California. When she isn't furiously scribbling away, Zoe enjoys Irish Dance, reading, Girl Scouts, horseback riding, MESA (Math, Engineering, Science Achievement) and being a kid.*

# Horse Of Stone

*by Zoe Appleby*

Atop a burnt hill
A horse does stand,
His proud head lifted,
Looking over the land.

He has stood there for ages,
Always alone,
For this great creature
Is a Horse of Stone.

The horse does watch
Throughout the night,
Yet only in the day
Is he in sight,
That Black Horse of Stone.

A saddle does lie
Upon his black hide,
Yet where is the rider,
Where is the guide
Of that Riderless, Black Horse of Stone?

Buffeted by wind,
Pounded by rain,
Yet the statue still does remain,
A Cold, Riderless, Black Horse of Stone.

Why he stands there
I do not know,
For 'tis only a place
Where burnt weeds grow.

He will stand there for ages,
Always alone,
Forevermore,
A Horse of Stone.

*Zoe Appleby is an eighth-grader attending Isbell Middle School in California. When she isn't furiously scribbling away, Zoe enjoys Irish Dance, reading, Girl Scouts, horseback riding, MESA (Math, Engineering, Science Achievement) and being a kid.*

# The Familiar Stranger

*by Bernadette Augello*

As the wind blew against my face, I could smell the sweet, sweet blood of humans nearby. I walked into the town and looked around. All the guys were staring at me. My black, curly, long hair blew in the wind. My eyes (for the moment) were caramel brown and my skin was as pale as the moon. I wore a black tank top with a black skirt and black high-heeled boots.

A different smell filled the air. I inhaled the scent, which was coming from the nearby wooded area. I followed it deep into the forest. The smell became bitter and strong. *A werewolf!* He was sitting on the ground leaning against a tree. I jumped in front of him and growled.

"I knew you would come to me," he said.

He had short black hair, green eyes, and mocha-colored skin. He was wearing a black tuxedo with a blue tie. He looked like he was in his thirties.

"What do you want?" I asked, not caring.

He stopped smiling and got serious. "I am Aiden, I –"

I cut him off. "Is it good or bad?" I asked, not looking at him.

"I just have something to tell you," he said. "Something your parents and I agreed upon."

"What?" I said, turning to face him. "What did you and my parents talk about?" I folded my arms across my chest.

"You are to marry my son," he said in a serious voice.

I burst out laughing. Tears fell down my face as I laughed. I wiped the tears away with my hand.

"Are you serious?" I asked, tilting my head to the side.

He gave me a look.

"Seriously? No!" I said. "I can't believe this at all!" *Why would my parents do this behind my back?* I thought.

"You will be staying at a mansion with my son, Prince Wolfgang."

I felt lightheaded.

"Here's a note that will give you the address," Aiden continued, handing me a folded-up slip of paper. I looked at the paper, then to him.

"Go on, take it," Aiden said, encouraging me. I reached out, then pulled back a little, still feeling wary of him. Finally I took the paper from his hand. There was my name, written out in sharp black letters. *This must really be happening*, I thought. I looked up, and Aiden was gone.

I unfolded the paper again and read: *To Mandy Willa Garden: The house will be next to the beach and forest near Skylight Town.* I folded up the paper and tucked it in my right boot. I ran back to my house with super-human speed.

"Mom! Dad!" I yelled.

"We're in here, darling!" my mother called. I marched into the living room. My parents were reading their books.

"What's the meaning of this?" I shouted at them. They both put down their books and stared at me.

"Meaning of what?" my mother asked, seeming genuinely confused.

"Why didn't you tell me I have to marry a werewolf?" I yelled.

The plant next to me burst into flames. My father ran to the other room and came back with a bucket of water. He splashed the plant and the fire went out.

My mother stared at me. Her dark blue eyes looked annoyed and angry.

"Tell me!" I insisted.

"We didn't tell you before because –" My mother stopped, and looked at my father.

"Because we knew that you wouldn't agree to this," my father continued as he stood next to my mom. I turned around to leave.

"Where are you going?" my father called after me.

"I'm not doing this," I said.

"You have to!"

I faced them. My mother's beautiful long, curly hair was pulled back from her face, revealing her dark blue eyes that were both sad and worried. My father's caramel brown eyes were angry, and his pale moon-white skin was like my own.

I didn't want my parents to be mad at me. I wanted them to be happy. I realized I had to marry this werewolf.

*Gross!* I thought. "Fine, I'll do it," I said under my breath.

I looked up at them and they were smiling.

"I'll pack my things," I said. My mom followed me to my room to help.

After I packed my clothes and everything I needed, we loaded all my stuff into our car and drove to the address on the slip of paper Aiden had given me.

We stopped at a huge gray house with black windows and a black door. The roof was black too. It was surrounded by a heavily wooded forest. There was a nearby beach with clear blue water and white sand that was dotted with seashells. We entered the house and the inside was nice. There was a black leather couch with a big flat-screen TV and two gray chairs. The walls were white and the floor was tan wood.

"So where's the mutt?" I asked, throwing my bag on a gray chair. I lay down on the black couch and stared at the ceiling. I heard footsteps on the staircase.

A guy my age stood in front of the stairs. He looked familiar, with his short brown hair, his beautiful dark blue eyes, his perfect lips, and the same mocha skin as Aiden. He was wearing a gray shirt, dark jeans and white sneakers. His eyes met mine.

"Mandy?" he asked.

"Yes?"

"It's me, Wolfgang, remember?" he said, smiling. I was lost for a minute. Then I remembered – we were friends a long time ago, in elementary school. *Wait, I'm supposed to marry my old friend, Wolfgang?* I thought.

"Wolfgang, you're a werewolf?" I asked, shocked.

"Ya didn't know?" he asked, tilting his head to the side.

"You're Aiden's son? I can't believe this."

"What about you?" he said. "My dad told me you're a vampire?"

"Yes," I said, tilting my chin up proudly.

Wolfgang came and sat next to me on the couch. We started talking and laughing. I found out his favorite color was dark blue, he loved chocolate and like me, he wanted to have a family. I smiled at him. "So, when's the wedding?" I asked.

"I'll have to ask my dad about it," he said.

We fell asleep on the couch. I opened my eyes to see Wolfgang with a big grin on his face.

"What are you so happy about?" I asked.

"You've been asleep a long time," he said.

"How long?"

"Three weeks. Today is our wedding day." He sounded excited.

I moaned and got up. I still felt tired. "What time is it?" I asked.

"We have a couple of hours till the ceremony, so you still have plenty of time to get ready," he said as he headed toward the door. "I'll be waiting in the living room with your parents."

I took a long, hot shower and wrapped a towel around me. I quickly blow-dried my hair and put on my wedding dress. It was beautiful: white like snow, with silver rose petals and sparkles. It was sleeveless and fit perfectly. I put on my gray eyeshadow, glitter on my cheeks, eyeliner, and red lipstick. I wore a tiara and veil and my silver heels. I walked downstairs, and my parents were there. They turned to look at me.

"Oh sweetie, you look beautiful!" my mother said, her voice filled with joy.

We went outside and got into the car. I felt nervous when we arrived at the church. My father and I stood together, preparing to walk down the aisle to the front of church where Wolfgang stood, handsome and waiting.

"Are you nervous?" my dad whispered to me.

"A little," I confessed.

The organist began to play the "Wedding March." My dad took my arm and we started walking. Everyone I knew was there. But my eyes were on Wolfgang. His brown hair was gelled back and he wore a black tuxedo with a white tie. I smiled at him and he smiled back. Before I knew it, I was there next to him staring into his dark ocean-blue eyes. My eyes filled with tears as we said our vows. Wolfgang lifted the veil and we kissed. Holding hands, we ran out of the church and into the black limo.

After our honeymoon, we went back to our gray house in the forest. Wolfgang slept but I was wide awake. I sighed happily and stared at the silver moon and stars. I smiled to myself and looked at the heart-shaped necklace that Wolfgang gave me on our honeymoon. *I guess marrying Wolfgang wasn't such a bad idea after all,* I thought, softly kissing Wolfgang's head. I was finally happy. I had found a place where I belonged.

Morning arrived and I left early to go hunting. I caught an elk and sank my teeth into its throat. Warm blood filled my mouth. After I finished eating, I got up and smelled the air.

*Werewolves?* I inhaled the scent deeply. *And vampires?* Vampires were near me.

Suddenly, I was tackled by a vampire with dark brown hair. His eyes were dark red and he was wearing a black T-shirt with jeans.

"I have a message," he whispered.

"Get off me!" I yelled, pushing him into a tree. I crouched down in attack mode.

"Relax," he said.

"What do you want?" I hissed.

"The vampires are going to war with the werewolves," he said.

"What?" I cried. He laughed darkly and ran away.

*What am I going to do?* I thought.

"Mandy!" I turned and Wolfgang was standing behind me. "Is it true?" he asked in a sad voice. "Are we really going to war?"

I just nodded my head and sat down on a log. He sat beside me.

"Wolfgang?" I whispered, not looking at him.

"Yes?" he asked.

"We're going to have a ... a baby."

*Bernadette Augello lives in New York with her family and enjoys writing fiction. She also loves reading – especially Twilight and other related books – movies, shopping, visiting and exploring little towns, and she loves pizza and Chinese food.*

# The Explosion

*by April Ball*

Stunned, I stood up. That could not just have happened. Sitting next to me, my brother looked to be in shock. I went to say something to him, but I realized I couldn't talk. I was too overcome with grief. I felt like I was being crushed. I let out a scream of agony. I couldn't breathe, and then it stopped: the feeling, the pain. I was stunned. My house, my parents, my belongings, now all in ashes.

The scene replayed in my mind. The blast. The explosion. My little brother and I had gone outside to get the mail. We were lucky. My brother was still sitting on the ground.

I started to cry. I cried and cried and cried. I couldn't stop. My neighbor rushed over. She stared, open-mouthed. "What happened?" she asked. "Are you kids okay? Who did this?"

"I don't know," I said. "Joey and I just walked out of the house and it happened."

My brother stood up. He was only seven and I was twelve. Where would we go? How would we live? Would we be sent to an orphanage?

Pretty soon neighbors from the entire block were in front of our house, gaping and gasping. Everybody was so intent on the explosion that nobody noticed Joey and me slipping out into the street. As we trudged along, Joey asked where we were going.

"No idea," I said, "but we can't stay here. I know that for sure."

It was growing dark. Joey complained that he was tired. That he wanted Mommy. I turned to him and said, "Joey, listen now and listen good. You saw the explosion. That wasn't fake. That wasn't one of your war video games. Our house, parents, belongings... everything is gone. Don't you get it? Mommy and Daddy aren't coming back. I know that in your war games your characters respawn back to life. Well, not here. This is real life and real life isn't as easy or as simple as pressing the triangle button on your controller. Your choices count, and so does your attitude. So be quiet and do what I tell you."

I gave Joey a hug and as I did, I felt a small tear drop on my arm. I couldn't tell if it was mine or not.

*April Ball is very excited about getting one of her stories published. She is ten years old and this is a huge accomplishment for her. She has extremely curly hair and adores cats. She loves acting and singing as well as writing.*

# Quiet, But Determined

*by Kaylin Barr*

I am quiet, but determined.
I wonder, can I ever be what I desire?
I hear them say I have no skill.
I see them shake their heads.
I want to be a writer.
I am quiet, but determined.

I pretend that I am famous.
I feel proud of my work.
I touch my keyboard, typing away.
I worry that I am no good.
I cry when people discourage me.
I am quiet, but determined.

I understand that it is a long, hard road.
I say, "All I can do is try."
I dream to one day be published.
I try to do my best.
I hope that someday it will be enough.
I am quiet, but determined.

*Kaylin Barr was born in Slockbridge, Georgia. She has always loved to read and write. Now, at the age of thirteen, she lives in Newnan, Georgia.*

# Humpback Whales

*by Nicole Bellmore*

When I was little, I used to go on whale-watching trips quite often, each time hoping to see one more whale than the last trip out. I've seen all different types of whales, but my favorite is the Humpback whale.

I love the way their tails move up and down instead of side-to-side. I love the way they breach – they are famous for that. Barnacles live on Humpback whales' skin and itch them, so they breach (jump out of the ocean and splash down on their backs) to try to get the barnacles off. I love the way they can live to be 95 years old. I love the way the Humpback whale looks. They can be four different colors ranging from white to gray, black to mottled. I think they look beautiful. I just love Humpback whales.

Some facts I have learned from my research are very fascinating. For example, did you know the Humpback whale has two blowholes? I thought all whales just have one. I also learned that Humpback whales maintain a body temperature of 100 degrees Fahrenheit at all times, unless they are ill.

Humpback whales are enormous, ranging from 42 to 62.5 feet in length. To give you an idea, that is as big as a school bus! A Humpback whale's heart is as big as a van. But do you know what's really amazing? These gentle giants *never* attack humans.

Humpback whales are wonderful creatures. I can't wait to go whale watching again!

*Nicole Bellmore lives in Ventura, California. She is eleven years old and loves the outdoors.*

# Nature's Beauty

*by Gianne Braza*

On spring days
the flowers and trees live again,
to show the beauty of
Earth's nature.

It blooms, filled with vivid colors and life.

On summer days
the sun kisses the world
with its rays of light, to show
Earth its radiance.

It shines, gleaming with vivaciousness.

On autumn days
the wind whispers to the
nature of Earth, how beautiful
the leaves of trees can be.

It changes, transforming in a unique way.

On winter days
the snows breathes its icy breath
on nature, turning Earth
into a winter beauty.

It is silent, fluffy white flakes descending
everywhere.

Earth is magnificent
and glorious.
From the soft, green grass
to the immensely blue sky,
nature is superlative.

*Gianne Braza is currently an eighth-grader in junior high school. She has written other works but this is the first time she has been published in an anthology.*

# Gymnastics Girls

*by Kassidy Broaddrick*

"But Mommy! I don't want to go!" Lily cried.

"You have to," her mother said calmly. "Now buckle your seatbelt." And they drove to the gym.

Lily, six years old, never wanted to go to gymnastics because she didn't like her coaches. It was the start of a new season and she hoped for a change.

"Mommy, who is that girl over there?" she asked.

"She looks like someone new. Why don't you go over and say hi?"

Lily skipped over to the new girl. She soon learned her name was Taylor and she was a year older than Lily. Soon enough, they were best friends. They made friendship bracelets and never wanted to take them off.

Years passed. When Lily was a freshman in high school, the girls tried out for their school's gymnastics team. They both made Varsity! Lily began to get noticed more and more from the top colleges in the state, while Taylor struggled to keep up. After the State Competition, Lily went on to Nationals. She won the gold in every event.

Soon after Lily turned sixteen came the Olympics. She had a shot to be the best of the best! She told Taylor the exciting news, but Taylor didn't seem thrilled.

"That's great for you, Lil," she said. But she didn't smile as she said it.

The Olympics came and Lily hadn't heard from Taylor in weeks. She was nervous about her gymnastics floor routine, and even more nervous than usual because she didn't have her best friend supporting her. She looked down at her wrist and saw the friendship bracelet she and Taylor had made so long before. She wondered if Taylor was watching the competition on TV.

Just then, cell her phone rang. It was Taylor. She apologized for acting so childish and jealous. "Just do your best, Lily," she said. "Go win that gold medal!"

Lily felt a boost of confidence. She did the best routines of her life because she knew she could be the best, and she had her best friend supporting her. She won the gold medal in the all-around competition! Taylor called once again and congratulated her.

After Lily finished high school, she decided to go to the University of Georgia on a gymnastics scholarship. They were rated number one in the country and Lily helped them keep it that way. And to think, she might not have done any of it without the encouragement and friendship Taylor gave her.

*Kassidy Broaddrick is an eighth-grade student at Sidney Middle School in Sidney, Ohio. She is active in cheerleading, gymnastics, choir and band.*

# Piper's Heart

*by Keely E. Brown*

The small yellow bird chirped happily, gracefully weaving her way through the branches, excited that she could finally go into town. Now that she was free from the nest that had held her prisoner for so long, she could do whatever she wanted.

*Wow*, was the only thought that went through her mind as she reached the edge of the forest, looking down onto the dirty streets leading into the massive town. In the distance, she could see a beautiful stone castle looming above everything else. She hopped onto the uneven cobblestone roads, looking around in amazement, when they waddled up to surround her. Pigeons. Mostly dull gray in color. But one pigeon stood out in particular, and he didn't look too happy. The green and purple feathers around his neck shone iridescently, and his beady orange eyes blazed with fire-like characteristics, as he stared angrily at the little yellow bird.

"Why are you here? Who are you? You are no pigeon!" he said, bobbing his head up and down as he looked around for more of her type.

"I'm Piper, and I'm visiting the town!" the young bird replied cheerfully. "And it's beautiful," she added, motioning towards the castle, her tiny black eyes shining brightly.

"Leave!" the angry pigeon retorted. "You're different, and you don't belong here!" By now, the other pigeons were moving closer, and Piper had caught on that they didn't like her. They were much bigger, and would hurt her if she didn't go away. But she was frozen with fear, and couldn't push off the ground to fly away. All she could do was close her eyes and wait for the pain to come.

But it never did. A little girl with tangled blonde hair, a dirt-smudged face, and old ragged clothes saved her life.

\* \* \*

This is how Piper described what had happened to her, as she sat in my cupped hands on the way back to the ramshackle building I called home. I didn't know what I would do with her – we could barely afford to feed my family, as it was – and even a bird as small as Piper would take up some of our food. And every bite counted when you were as poor as we were. But I wouldn't have been able to live with myself had I let this beautiful little songbird get injured by the pigeons.

When I walked in the front door and showed Mother, she had a fit. She wasn't going to let a bird stay inside the house. I didn't understand why – our house was already filthy; having a single bird inside wouldn't make a difference.

"Absolutely not, Alys," Mother told me. Which I thought was ridiculous. Piper was just a bird, only a little bigger than my fist. But Mother probably thought that I was being ridiculous, to care so much about a bird.

*Fair enough*, I thought, making my way into my tiny bedroom, only slightly larger than a cupboard. *Doesn't mean I have to listen to her, though*. The bed lay in one corner – a sack of straw – and next to it was a small nightstand, made of maple, that Father built for me when I was little. I pulled out the drawer, and set Piper into it after putting in some of the straw from my bed. No one ever came into my room, so they wouldn't have to know that I'd kept the bird after all.

After a few months, however, Mother became suspicious. I'd been saving a little bit of my meal every night for Piper, which wasn't like me. I usually ate all that I could. But I didn't want the little bird to go out hunting for food, because I had no idea if she knew how to hunt. She *was* only a songbird. And there were still those pigeons out there, too. I didn't know what I would do if she didn't return. Piper was only a bird, but I was attached. She was my friend.

"You better not have that bird... I told you not to keep her," Mother told me sternly one night, when I tried to sneak back into my room with a small piece of bread.

"Of course not," I replied, avoiding her eyes.

The next day, I picked the yellow bird up, remembering how I got her. She was now much bigger than before, and her adult feathers were completely grown in. I sighed. "Piper, you need to go. Mother's suspicious that I have you, and if she finds out, she'll wring your neck before I can get you safely out of here." Opening the window, I held out my hand so that she could fly away. But it wasn't safe anywhere, unless she went back to the trees that she had originally come from. And I didn't think that she wanted to. Soldiers patrolled the streets, and everyone knew that war was coming, even if they didn't tell us.

"But I love you. You saved me," the little bird piped, cocking her head as she hopped onto the windowsill. I didn't say anything, just closed the window, making her jump into the air to avoid being flattened. I walked out the room, looking back to see a little yellow speck flying away, towards the castle. And that was that. I didn't expect to ever see Piper again. Didn't expect to hear her sweet voice as she sang, or feel her soft golden feathers. She was gone.

As I lay in bed that night, trying to fall asleep, I caught myself staring out the window, wanting to see Piper flying back to me. And I did. At first, I thought I was just imagining things, but as she flew closer and tapped her orange beak on the glass, I knew that it was really Piper. Gasping, I opened the window and let her in. She looked scared, and I wondered what had happened, but before I could ask, she told me. "There are soldiers not too far from here, Alys. I was resting on a branch, and they thought I was a spy. They tried to shoot me with an arrow. Oh, it was *terrifying*! I think they're coming *here*, and soon!"

I stared at her, dumbfounded. Piper *could* make a good spy. Hurriedly, I wrote a short note on a piece of parchment and tied it to her foot with a flexible piece of straw. "Fly to the castle," I said. I pretty much shoved her out the window and she flew off. This time, though, I expected Piper to return, and I didn't care if Mother found out about her.

Throughout the next couple weeks, Piper was our spy, telling the town where the army was, how many soldiers there were, and what type of weapons they had. By the time they arrived, expecting to ambush us, the King had gathered together a pretty large army – we were a big town – and now war raged on around us.

*If it weren't for Piper, we wouldn't be winning this fight right now*, I thought. She really was an extraordinary bird. Mother had finally accepted her into our family, and right now, we were all waiting anxiously for her to return from another mission, for the King himself.

When Piper flew through the open window, she looked terrible. Feathers were missing, and she had accidentally flown too low and been sliced by a sword. I knew she wouldn't make it.

She rested in my cupped hands, as she did on that day I'd found her so long ago. Her breathing was ragged. She was fading. "If those pigeons could see you now, they'd want to go back in time and give you

29

the chance that you deserved, Piper," I said, trying to comfort her. She didn't answer. I gently stroked the top of her feathery head, trying to think of what else to say. Then she went limp in my hands, and I cried.

* * *

My family and I were outside, along with everyone else in the town, celebrating our victory and the war being over. Even the King was there. Piper had really helped us out, and I wished that she were with us more than anything. I think my little sister could tell that I still missed Piper, because she skipped over to me and pointed to the dark night sky.

"See that, Alys?" she said. "That little group of stars over there is Piper. And that big reddish star – that's her heart. Because she loved you enough to risk her life and save you and the entire kingdom."

Honestly, I didn't know my sister had such wisdom in her. She was an eight-year-old! But I did value her words. I could almost hear the small bird's melodious voice, feel her soft golden feathers. Now I knew that Piper would always be with us, watching over my family and the kingdom. I ruffled my sister's hair, and smiled, suddenly feeling a whole lot better.

*Keely Brown is an eighth-grade student in Houston, Texas. She lives with her mom, dad, older and younger brothers, and dog named Bagel. Besides writing, she enjoys art and band, and her primary instrument is the oboe.*

# Socks

*by Taylor Busse*

I was only five years old: the age of princesses and fairy tales, dolls and microwavable mac n' cheese. Little girls my age liked to have friends over and play make-believe and get dressed up for pretend tea parties. Not me. I had one best friend who was all I ever wanted or needed. He was my cat, Socks. I loved Socks, and I'm pretty sure he loved me back. We were inseparable.

"Mama! Mama! Look! His socks are white!"

That's what I thought at the time: that the scrawny stray cat was actually wearing white socks. In addition to his white paws, there were bold grey and black markings in his back. His tail resembled a raccoon's tail: grey with dominant black rings. Socks only had half a tail. Some people found it strange, but I would just grin and say, "That's how he's supposed to be! He's special." And I was right. Socks certainly had character.

"That's gonna be his name! Socks! And he will be my best friend forever!"

"No, no, no way!" my mother protested. "We do NOT want him in our house! C'mon, April! Don't touch him! He's probably covered in fleas!"

We all know what happened next. I burst into tears, the desperate tantrum that only an upset five-year-old with a broken heart can produce.

"I want him!" I said, stomping my feet into the ground. "I need him!"

Many tears later, my mother finally gave up and let me bring Socks home. Before long, he was part of the family.

"C'mon Socks! We're gonna play on the swing set," I said, running outside into the backyard. "You know that one day ... one day, we're gonna be FAMOUS! Did you know that Socks? You and me. We'll be in all the movies." I gave him my most diva-styled pose.

Socks just looked at me as I swayed back and forth on the blue swing.

"It's gonna be so fun. Everyone will wanna meet us and get our autographs."

Socks cocked his head slightly, as if to say, "Sure, April, why not?"

"You like that idea?" I asked.

Socks got up to his feet and arched his back to stretch. Then he leapt onto my lap while I swayed on the swing. I stared into his emerald eyes shaped like almonds.

"Well, let's wait on that," I said to him. "For right now, it's okay just like this. Don't you think? Just you and me … me and you."

* * *

"Hey, April! Can you come down here? Today is your big day and I want to show you something!"

"I'm coming! What do you want, Dad?" I asked in a tired, grouchy tone I didn't normally use with my father. "It's so late! Or is it early?"

"It's 12:01! It's your birthday, April! It's April 13th!" he said in an annoyingly cheery voice for past midnight.

"Well, can we celebrate in, like, eight hours? I'm a teenager and I need my beauty sleep!"

"I want to show you something!" my dad said again. "You might think I'm crazy though."

"Knew that a long time ago," I joked.

We stepped outside onto the porch. It was dark and pouring rain. Thunder rattled the house and lightning cracked the sky right down the middle, like breaking an egg.

We sat on the porch for a few moments, listening to the rain tapping the roof and plinging in the gutter. It was dark, chilly and misty – but in a pleasant way.

I looked over at my father. His five o'clock shadow needed shaving and his flannel shirt reminded me of a farm. It's what he wore every day: jeans with holes and a flannel shirt.

"Look very closely at the woods," he said, pointing a finger towards the trees Socks and I used to romp through when I was a little girl. "Watch as the lightning strikes."

Seconds later, I was mesmerized. For a split second I felt like I was in a dream, a different universe. I realized my dad wasn't crazy at all. A long bolt of lightning struck behind the trees followed by thunder and another flash of lightning. The sky transformed to a deep, dark ocean blue. The trees were dark shadows, like a still-life painting. The whole scene was so simple, so pretty yet haunting all at once. It sent chills up my spine.

"It's so much different at night," I whispered.

"I know," my dad said. "I've always loved the rain, so I come out here a lot when there's a storm. It calms me. I thought it would be a nice place to talk."

"What about?"

"April, you're fifteen now. I never imagined how fast fifteen years could go. I feel like all I did was blink, and suddenly you're practically grown up. You're not gonna need me much longer. You're gonna leave me someday."

"What are you talking about?" I said. "I'm always going to need you."

"You're not always going to be my little girl."

"Sure I will, Dad."

"No, no you won't. Eventually I will give you away at your wedding to somebody else who claims they love you more than anyone or anything in the world. But I hope you know that I will always love you and I will always be here for you, no matter what."

"I know."

"Sorry, I guess this is a lot to throw at you this late at night. I've just been thinking. I wish we still had the relationship we had when you were a kid. I miss that time."

His eyes started to get teary, and I felt my eyes water, too. "I'll always be your little girl," I said.

"I know inside you will be," he replied, hugging me. "It's just that you're so big and grown now. I feel like we've drifted apart a bit and I'm afraid of losing you. I love you, April. I know I don't say it as often as I should."

"I love you too, Dad. And I promise that the day I walk down the aisle won't be for a long time yet. Plus, nobody could ever replace you. You're my one and only father." I smiled. "And I always like talking to you, even at 12:30 in the morning."

"Yeah, it is really nice spending time like this together," my dad said. "I just wanted to show you what many people overlook, even though it's right in front of them."

"You and me, Dad," I said.

"Me and you," he agreed.

Right then, lightning struck and once again I was mesmerized.

\* \* \*

"Amazing," he said to me. "We've been married for thirty years and every year has been a wonderful journey with you, April. Happy anniversary."

"Happy anniversary," I said to my husband. "The party was a really fun time." All four of our children and nine of our grandchildren had been there, laughing and having fun together. Many of our friends showed up also, creating a wonderful day of memories.

"The day isn't over yet," my husband said. "Your father gave me a brilliant idea for a gift."

"But we both agreed not to give each other presents!"

"I couldn't resist. I think you'll like this one."

Before I could protest more, he disappeared into the garage. Moments later he came back with the most unexpected gift.

"You didn't!" I exclaimed.

"Oh, but I did. For you," he said, handing me a fragile little kitten with white paws.

"He's beautiful, and just what I wanted!"

"You wanted a kitten? Really?"

"I did – I just didn't know it until right now!" I laughed. "And look! He's got socks on!"

We agreed that Socks was the perfect name. Then the three of us went out to the porch and watched the thunderstorm. On my lap, Socks looked up at me and stretched.

"You and me, little guy," I said softly. I swore Socks smiled. I'm pretty sure he did.

*Taylor Busse is an eighth-grader at Sidney Middle School in Sidney, Ohio. An honor-roll student, she participates in band and loves soccer and fast-pitch softball. During Mr. Stolly's class this year she has written several stories and found a real interest in writing.*

# Take My Hand

## by Lucia Kemeng Chen

### Scotland, 1189

Simon Darnell was six years old when he met his first Scotsman and fought his first fight. Kennan Maclachlan was of the same age when he met his first Englishman and fought... well, suffice to say, it was far from his first fight.

It started during the Border Festival, one of the few peaceful days in an age of war and unrest. The Scottish and English would stomach the sight of each other for three entire weeks while enjoying grand feasts and competitions. But the animosity never faded.

So when the wiry English boy toppled the makeshift fortress of twigs and stones Kennan had spent the past hour constructing, the latter decided to retaliate.

Naturally, Kennan, having the greater strength and experience, swiftly overpowered the small and skinny Simon. But Simon was as stubborn as he was proud, and it wasn't long before Kennan was down in the dirt, spewing out lumps of mud.

That was when the fight truly began. Punches and kicks were heavily meted out as the two boys brawled. A solid punch to Simon's jaw finally brought him crumpling to the ground. Simon squeezed his eyes shut, waiting for the next blow. A moment passed. Then two.

When he finally deemed it safe to crack open an eyelid, Simon was astonished to see an outstretched hand. His opponent had a smile on his face and a trace of laughter in his greenish-gold eyes.

"Come on, take my hand," the Scot said. When Simon didn't budge, he added, "Yer not afraid are yeh, English?"

"'Course not!" Simon cried out indignantly. "You should be the one that's afraid, cos I can make your left eye just as purple as your right!"

The Scot laughed. "Yer not bad for an English." He pulled Simon to his feet. "I'm Kennan, future laird of the Maclachlan clan," he announced pompously.

Simon shook his outstretched hand. "And I'm Simon, future... uh... future soldier," he concluded. "I'm going to fight in King John's army."

"Ha! Papa says he can take down King John with one hand tied behind his back!"

"I bet I can take *you* down with both hands tied behind my back!"

"Want to try?" Kennan threatened, the fire returning to his eyes. Simon was already lunging for his throat. Within seconds, the boys were again rolling on the ground.

"Peace! Peace!" Kennan finally called out.

"Too scared, Scot?" Simon taunted.

"No, it's just that Mother's making mincemeat pie, and I want to get to the cottage before Alec eats it all." Kennan was halfway down the hill before he turned back. "D'yeh want to come for supper?"

"No way! I – " Simon began before his stomach let out a loud growl. He looked up at a smirking Kennan. "Well, I s'pose I can bear with you a little while longer if I'm getting mincemeat pie."

And so a friendship began.

### 1193

*Dear Simon,*

*Papa says we kinnah be friends no more. He says I kinnah talk to you 'less you start speaking Gaelic and wearing plaid. Seeing as yer English, I dinnah think that's happening very soon.*

*Good-bye,*
*Kennan*

### 1206

*Friend,*

*Should our armies ever clash, know one thing: I will not raise my sword against you.*

*Sir Simon Darnell of King John's Army*

## *1212*

"We've caught another one, Laird Kennan."

"Aye, Cormag," Kennan Maclachlan said as he accepted the warrior's sword and strode down the hill. "Those Englishmen have been coming in droves lately. Blasted nuisances."

"Gavyn wanted to do the beheading, but I thought you might want to, being laird and all," Cormag remarked.

Kennan groaned. In truth, he hated beheading – English or otherwise. But what Cormag said was true; he was laird, and the clan always came first.

Cormag led him to where Gavyn waited with the bound soldier. Kennan tightened his hold on the sword and inhaled sharply, dreading the duty before him.

That was when the Englishman turned to face him.

Kennan dropped the sword, his lips inadvertently tugging upward. "Simon."

"Thank God, Kennan! Thought I was going to be beheaded back there." Simon's relief was starkly evident.

"Keep yer mouth shut, English. Yer pollutin' the Highland air," Gavyn growled.

"An' don't yeh be speakin' to the laird like that," Cormag spat.

Kennan frowned. "Gavyn, Cormag –"

"For heaven's sakes Laird, if yer not going to behead him soon, I'd be happy to do the duty," Gavyn interjected.

"That won't be necessary," Kennan said, staring at the sword on the ground. The clan. The clan always came first. Hands shaking, he bent to retrieve the sword. Then, eyes trained on the ground, he strode toward Simon.

But before he swung, Kennan made the mistake of looking into his old friend's eyes, and the mix of sadness and resignation he saw there made him pause mid-swing.

"The clan comes first, Kennan," Simon whispered.

"Aye, it does," Kennan murmured. He slashed his sword through the ropes binding Simon's wrists and ankles. "And I'm going to do the Maclachlan clan a great service today by sparing them from the sight of blood."

"What in God's name are yeh doin'?" Cormag bellowed. "He's an Englishman!"

"Yer commitin' an act of betrayal!" Gavyn's voice was vehement.

"No, I'm committing an act of friendship," Kennan announced in a steely tone that silenced his men.

"Take my hand," he said to Simon. "Unless yer afraid?"

Simon chuckled as he accepted Kennan's proffered hand. "You should be the one that's afraid, cos I can make your left eye just as purple as your right."

"Want to try?"

"I think I'll settle for some mincemeat pie. I have yet to find someone who makes it better than your mama."

"Laird?" Cormag ventured, an uneasy expression on his face.

"Aye, Cormag. Tell Cook to set an extra place at the table. We have a special guest tonight."

Cormag and Gavyn were left gaping in disbelief as the two friends – one Scottish, one English – strolled down the hill.

*Lucia Chen is a sophomore in high school. When she's not writing, she enjoys holing up at the library with a good book or running with her high school's cross country team. In addition to short stories, Lucia has dabbled in poetry and is currently at work on her first novel. She lives in Michigan with her mom, dad, and little brother.*

# What Makes You Happy?

*by Korina Chilcoat*

Oh, little girl? What makes you happy?
Is it pink cotton candy or blue ponies?
Bubblegum trees or clouds made of glitter?
Is it a song playing in the background?
Is it a treasure chest filled with diamond tiaras?
Oh, please tell me what makes you happy!

Is it a pair of red ballet shoes?
Or could it be the finest tea in all of England?
Is it walking up the Eiffel Tower at night, while lights
sparkle from the beams?
Is it fairies who grant your wishes?
Or is it leprechauns who dance for you in the fields
of youth?
Oh, please tell me what makes you happy!

Is it a carriage filled with roses, posies, and tulips?
Or is it to be princess of the land of magic?
Is it a ruby-encrusted wand that guides you to your true love?
Or could it even be a trip down a river on a lily pad?
Is it the emerald ring found in the depths of the forest of Kilanroo?
Oh, please tell me what makes you happy!

Is it a handsome prince who gives you sweet sugar kisses?
Or is it a book – the best fairytale ever written?
Is it sunny days filled with picnics and maypoles?
Or is it a starry night with the moon shining above?
Oh, please tell me what makes you happy!

So I know how to be that happy once again.

*Korina Chilcoat is seventeen years old and a senior in high school. She also is an early admit student in college, president of her 4H District and County Councils, co-reporter for her FBLA District, and head editor for the Library Section of her school's newspaper. In her free time she loves to write about anything and everything.*

# Paper Cut

## *by Bethany Dean*

I leave my words on this paper.
I leave my thoughts, my feelings,
My deepest desires.

I leave everything I have to this paper.
I've lost everything I had to this paper;
My emotions, my secrets, my torment.

I can't speak in person but I can write on paper.
I can tell you how much I hate you,
Despise you... love you.

This paper ignites the demon words within.
This paper calls down my Heavenly thoughts
And leaves them for everyone to see.

What I can't say, this paper reveals.
I strive to find a different release but all I
Find is blood, sweat, and tears.

Red ink drops and stains this paper.
It is my momentary lapse and loss of control;
Like twinkling rubies it dances on the canvas.

The sweat from aching fingers stains this paper.
As I struggle for words and gasp for breath
The sweat moistens, smudges, and reveals.

These tears ruin this paper.
This is no place for actions or sorrow;
It's for the words, for the pen, for the desperate.

I hate this paper and what it stands for:
My inability to speak, my inability to
Be real, truthful, and honest in person.

Words hurt more on paper.
Words can be fixed and clearly stated,
But speech can be misheard... never heard.

This paper is a tomb for my words.
This paper refuses to be cremated.
When the ink runs dry only then will the words
die.

I leave my words on this paper.
I leave my heart, my hate, my love.
I leave everything I have... to this paper.

*Bethany Dean is not only an avid reader and writer, she is also a dancer and self-taught musician. She enjoys having plants but can't seem to keep them alive. Bethany is currently writing her second book; the first has yet to be edited because she despises editing.*

# Fall Dreams

*by Robyn Dickason*

I sit by the windowsill and yawn,
and watch yellow, red, and orange leaves
twirl from the branches,
drift in the air,
and land on the soggy earth.
I thrust open the window,
letting in a cool draft.
I smell something special in the air.
Fall is here
and it fills me with delight.

The rakes will soon be released to do their job,
to sweep large piles around the yard.
When a mound is big enough,
I will take a step back, then leap.
The damp leaves will cling to my winter jacket,
as I work once again to fix the pile,
and then...
I will hop once more.
Mom will make hot cocoa as the sky darkens early.
I will sip my drink, near the fire,
enjoying the burn on my tongue,
the singe down my throat.

Yes, this surely is fall, I think,
as I wrap my scarf 'round my neck
and see jack-o-lanterns' eerie smiles on the porch.
I strap on my boots,
grab the rakes,
and step into the crisp fall air.

*Robyn Dickason is a thirteen-year-old homeschooler.
She enjoys reading, sports, writing, marine biology,
and babysitting. She is the second-oldest of five.*

# The "Not So Spy" Life

*by Laurie Drell*

Karen Gray walked across the street to meet up with her friends Lizzie and Cameron for their weekly coffee session. The Starbucks stop had been going on almost every Monday morning since the three friends were freshmen at Wimberley High School. They were all juniors now, and Karen had learned that a tall mocha frappuccino every week with your two best friends sure helped keep your stress level down – especially during the AP-testing, college-prepping craziness of junior year.

As much as Karen loved her two best friends and Wimberley – a small town just a couple hours away from Austin, Texas – she wasn't sure she wanted to live in Texas forever. She wanted to travel and make her own exciting, new adventures.

You see, Karen's parents were spies. You know, like in the CIA?

But Karen's mother didn't want her daughter to have a "spy" life. She wanted a "normal" life for her baby girl. So, when Karen was born, Mrs. Gray quit her job at the Callaghan Academy for Exceptional Young Women, settled down in Wimberley, and became a European history teacher at Wimberley High School.

"I've always wondered what it would be like," Karen confessed to Lizzie and Cameron as they waited for their coffees.

"What would be like?" Cameron asked.

"Being a spy."

"I know what you mean," Lizzie agreed. "We've lived in Wimberley for almost seventeen years. I could use a change."

"I actually like it here," Cameron said. "Despite that old saying, I think the truth is that the grass is *not* always greener on the other side."

* * *

Karen pulled into the school parking lot, shutting off the latest Taylor Swift hit playing on the car radio. She noticed a new student. A guy. He was cute. Brown hair, brown eyes, tall. Karen stepped out of her car and shouldered her backpack.

The mysterious boy walked towards the front office. Karen had never seen him before, and Wimberley was a small school. *Maybe he's transferring in the middle of the semester?* Karen thought. She didn't have much experience with boys, but this guy looked nice. And if he was a new student, it was likely he didn't know anyone at school. So Karen decided to talk to him. Even though she wasn't really a spy, this could be her first "mission."

*Mission One: Activated.*

"Hey, are you new to Wimberley? My name's Karen. I'm a junior here. Nice to meet you."

"Hi, yeah I'm new. I need to go to the front office. Am I going the right way?"

"Yeah, it's across the courtyard. I can take you there. What's your name?"

"Zach."

"Nice to meet you, Zach. What year are you?"

"I'm a junior. I just moved here from Washington D.C."

"It's a lot warmer down here in Texas."

"Sure is."

*Zach clearly is not a big talker,* Karen thought. *Or maybe he's just shy because he doesn't know me.*

When Zach and Karen walked into the front office, Zach got his schedule and the regular school forms.

"That's cool," Karen said, peeking over his shoulder at his schedule. "We have Algebra II, fourth period, together. I can help you find your classes if you want."

"Thanks... Karen? It's Karen, right?"

"Yep. Karen Gray."

Zach smiled. "I'm really glad we met."

*Mission One: Complete.*

*Laurie Drell is a seventeen-year-old high school student from Houston, Texas. She enjoys writing, photography, reading, and cooking.*

# Lyrical Fragments

## by Lily Elderkin

"Oh, *no.*"

It's my mother, in the other room, sobbing. Why is she crying? She called her friend Naomi almost two hours ago just to chat. Now she's *crying*?

"Mom?" I whisper, walking in. She's wiping her face with a tissue. "What is it?"

She holds up a finger, as if to tell me Naomi is way more important than *me*, her only child, the screw-up who acts too much like her sister, my Aunt Sara.

Aunt Sara ran away, so many years ago, and I know that it hurts my mother to see me wear her old clothes and root for the college basketball team she loved so much. She's never come back – not a word to any of us. She was nearly fifteen years younger than my mother. I was three when she left. My grandparents were heartbroken. Still are, actually.

I wonder, sometimes, what it would be like to have your beloved little girl run away.

I cast my mother an angry glance, and then hurry out of the room. I'm not a Good Girl, as my mother tries to make me. My father tells her to let me be, that I'll grow my own way.

I rush up to my room, rip my guitar from its case and pull out my stand from beneath my bed. The only thing that can calm me is music: the rhythmic chords and the endless strain of lyrics – chorus, bridge, start, finish. I lightly strum, humming to myself. There is one lyric that hasn't left my mind all week, and I so, so want to – desperately *need* to – make a song out of it, or at least a refrain.

*Cinderella has her happy ending,*
*Prince Charming swept her off her feet.*

It's a promising beginning, and I even have the tune to it. But no more than those two lines, which I scrawl down in a rose-pink notebook bought for me by my mother when I was still young enough to accept her presents. I've filled it with half-thoughts, fragments, full songs, and doodles that are more embarrassing to me than reading back my songs. I call the song "Fairy Tales" and stare at the page for a moment, humming.

I bite down on my lip and take out an old, tattered music book from my shelf, filled with Broadway classics that I can't get enough of. I begin to sing, my fingers taking over without even flipping to the correct page. Eyes shut, I have entered nirvana, taking with me the beauty of my music, the love of performance and the haunting melodies coming from my old, frail guitar.

I hear my mother sniffle, "Goodbye," so pitiful that I almost falter. But no, I've played this song too many times. I know it by heart now. My fingers won't let me stumble; my vocal chords refuse to stop.

And then, with one last heart-throbbing note, I finish and come down from my high, breathing deeply at the power of the music that I can make. I set my guitar back in its case, gently. I close the book and put it back on my shelf, making a mental note to tape the binding, *again*.

I head downstairs, my stomach rumbling and my mouth watering at the smell of my mother beginning her cooking.

I don't even need to ask when I walk into the kitchen. She knows I am curious, and I know she wants a sympathetic ear and a shoulder to lean on.

She sniffs loudly and says, "Naomi has cancer."

I close my eyes against an onslaught of tears of my own. Naomi – my godmother, nearly my aunt – has been there since the day I was born and is one of the most understanding women I know.

"But – but Naomi can fight it. Right? I mean, this is *Naomi* we're taking about, the woman who fought off a dog attack. Right? Right, Mom?"

I want her reassurance so badly that it nearly kills me to see her shut her eyes forcefully and shake her head, her chin wobbling. "No, baby, this might be it."

She opens her arms and I hug her, so tightly, because no matter how Sara-like I am, and no matter how she tries to control my life, we are united in this daunting, terrifying grief.

\* \* \*

I do not play again for weeks afterwards. There is no music left in me – or in the dying body of Naomi.

"Play... for me... Celine. Please..." she says one day as I sit beside her hospital bed. Her eyes are closed and her hands, clutching mine, are so frail.

"Naomi, I don't have my guitar," I say softly.

"Sing, Celine... My angel... sing..."

So I do as I'm told, because I always have, and if a dying woman wants to hear my voice, then she *will* hear it.

I sing the Broadway songs that I've memorized, a Beatles tune that will remind Naomi of her childhood, and then I say, "I'm going to sing you a song that I wrote. If you don't want to hear it, just tell me to stop."

Lightly, so lightly that I can barely feel it, she squeezes my hand. I sing her the Cinderella song, "Fairy Tales," making it up as I go along, tapping out the beat on her hand and getting into it, really feeling the music like I haven't been able to since Naomi got sick.

It's getting more personal than I expected, and I find myself creating a stanza for Aunt Sara, and many more for Naomi.

And I think she knows it, even if I don't name names.

"That... was... excellent..." she gasps to me, and I blush and shake my head.

"Shhh, Naomi, don't strain yourself."

"I... need you... to know... about... your aunt... Sara loved you... so... much, Celine... like her... own... daughter... and she... misses you... I know... she... does, angel... because... I will... miss you... too."

I'm stunned, but I tell her to shush. Why is she hurting herself for me? She tells me, all in one ragged gasp – "It's her message to you, her love and her devotion."

And then Naomi lays back on the bed, message delivered, her frail body shaking as she breathes shallowly.

"'Bye," I say, kissing her forehead and squeezing her limp hand one last time.

\* \* \*

Naomi dies, less than a month later. Such a short illness. I can't believe how quickly things move: she dies on a Saturday, her wake is the coming Monday, and then her funeral is that very Tuesday.

I'm so tired of grief, I decide, sitting beside my mother as she helps to plan the funeral. "Food – we have to feed them..." she says, so wearily.

"I don't understand why she'd want all this," says Naomi's son, Daniel, staring blankly at her documented-and-signed last wishes. "Why would she want an open casket? To hurt us all?"

"Dan, it's what she wanted," his aunt says softly.

"It doesn't make sense! Mom wouldn't want this stuff!" he says, his face a sickly pale yellow even as his cheeks redden with fury. He stands and runs up the stairs.

Daniel is my age, a good friend, but for the first time in my life, I do not understand what he is going through. Our mothers were the common thread in our relationship; they'd get together and do yoga in one of our living rooms when our friends came over, or they'd sing karaoke at a school fundraiser together, laughing so hard that neither of them could breathe. We were simultaneously embarrassed and amused by our mothers, and now – now I have my mother, and Dan is alone.

I want to go upstairs and find him, tell him I wish I understood, or play him a song, but I can't bear to. I don't have the courage to see him cry again. Instead, I bury my face in my mother's shoulder, so grateful to have her.

"She would like that Dan is opening up," someone says in a lame attempt to comfort us or cover the silence, or both.

I get chills, and I can't figure out why, until I realize we're using Naomi's name in the past tense. Her life is in the past tense now, and it rattles me.

Suddenly, Naomi's daughter, Clara, a twenty-year-old business-minded girl who is nothing like her mother, takes charge. "I'll order the food – where should we get it from? Oh, I know – that pizza place on the corner of Lake and Imperial is fine. Celine, go online and print us a menu."

I stand and go to the computer downstairs, grateful for Clara and her no-nonsense attitude. I couldn't do it, couldn't be so... *tough*. And I think that Naomi would be so, so proud of her daughter, for staying herself.

Clara hasn't cried since her mother died.

\* \* \*

"Mom," I ask tentatively, that night, knowing her tears have dried up for a moment, "how well did Aunt Sara and Naomi know each other?"

She's too sad to be bristly about the mention of Aunt Sara. "Oh, *years*. Naomi and I babysat for her when we were younger. Sara is Clara's godmother, and such a *good* one she is," she says bitterly.

"Could they still be in contact?"

"No, no, *no*, darling. Naomi would have told me, and Sara wouldn't have done that to me. She knows better."

Yes, my mother is too fragile to be played with. Perhaps they were talking, and Naomi hadn't told my mother for precisely that reason.

I swipe at my wet eyes and go up to my room, fingering my guitar. I haven't picked it up since Naomi got diagnosed, and it feels so foreign.

I never thought I would feel that way about my beloved instrument. I open my rose-colored notebook, eager to play something. I see the "Fairy Tale" song, just the first two lines, and struggle to recall the words I sang for Naomi, but I can only remember a little bit: the part about Aunt Sara.

*...and I feel betrayed.*

Just that one line, and none of the stanzas about Naomi. I feel wretched, and toss my guitar down. Putting my head in my hands, I wish for inspiration.

Does grief suck every ounce of creativity you have left and wash it away with the tears? Do those dehydrated headaches push away the songs inside me? Does sadness feed on you, eating up your happy thoughts and imagination, leaving behind a life of crying and aching hearts?

\* \* \*

"I was talking to her last night."

Those are my mother's first words as she pours herself a cup of coffee the morning of the wake.

"What do you mean, Mom?" I ask, afraid to hear her answer.

"Naomi was talking to me. I can't remember specifically what we said – it was more of a spiritual thing. You would have liked to have been there, Celine."

My father puts his arm around her, and she hugs him to her tightly.

"We'll pick you up from school at one," Dad tells me. I go off to the bus, feeling so separated from my classmates. They laugh and talk, but I stare blankly ahead of me, my thoughts filled with the white of Naomi's skin when she stopped breathing and the peaceful set of her mouth.

*At peace*, she seemed to tell us.

But *at peace* is such a difficult thing to think about when I'm greedy and want her back, to be the aunt I lost when I was so young.

My eyes do not tear up, thankfully, for the duration of the school day, but I cannot focus. Over and over, my teachers come up to me and say, "I'm so sorry about your aunt," because Dad e-mailed them all.

It's easier to say she's an aunt than "mother's friend," because that does not reflect the love, the connection. Not at all.

I leave halfway through math, feeling half-self-conscious and half-mysterious as I shut the door silently behind me and head down the hall, where my impatient, puffy-eyed mother stands.

She picks up my little sister, Alexi, at her elementary school and then my father at home, and we meet Naomi's family in a cold, gray building nearby. Clara looks strong and resolute, while Dan is crying into her shoulder. Their father won't meet anyone's eyes.

We enter, and I look at the floor as I walk towards the casket at the front of the big room. I can't look at it, half afraid and half unwilling, still, to believe she's actually gone.

We are treated like family members; my mother as Naomi's sister and Alexi and I as her nieces. The people who work here all say how sorry they are that we have lost a loved one, but I feel it's sort of a sham – how many times do they say that per day? Do they imagine the lives of the deceased? Count the number of people who arrive to see who *was* the most popular?

I can't imagine working at a place this gloomy.

* * *

When I finally get the courage to look upon Naomi's face, it scares me. Her smile is small and insincere. I think of the poor people who have to make every corpse look like that, so strange and unlike themselves.

They've trimmed her hair so her split-ends are gone, and her face is an orangey color that comes from too many tanning salons or too much makeup. Her fingernails are a short, sensible length, *nothing* like how they were in life. I place my fingers over hers, which are crossed over her chest like in a horror movie. She doesn't look peaceful – she looks empty.

"It's not really her," Dan tells me, from behind, surprising me. "She's gone. This is just her stupid body that betrayed us all."

Strangely poetic, for an adolescent boy.

"I know," I say, and remove my hand from hers. I feel sick as I see the makeup that has rubbed off onto my fingers. I don't have the heart to show it to Dan, so I rub it off on my nice black slacks and pretend to be composed. "I know exactly what you mean."

We stay for hours, obligated to receive everyone's sentiments. Some people pray over Naomi's body. Others browse the old photographs of her we've put up on display.

I wonder what Naomi would think of all the fuss: "Oh, your aunt was such a sweet woman, charming and loving and so very full of life..."; "Undoubtedly she'd appreciate you being here, dear..."; "I will remember her always because of..." such-and-such memory.

It lasts for so long that I wish I could just go home, but there isn't anything left in me when we finally *are* allowed home. I collapse on my bed, and just as I am drifting off, my mother comes in, swiping at her eyes.

"Darling, will you play tomorrow?" she asks. I open my eyes and look at her blankly.

"You want me to have *fun* tomorrow?" I repeat, stunned.

"Oh no, play – you know, guitar. For the funeral. Naomi *so* loved the way you played and sang." She sits on the edge of my bed and squeezes my feet, like she used to when I was very small.

"All right, Mom," I agree, sighing. "What?"

She sniffs mightily. "Amazing Grace?"

I nod, already half-asleep again. "Okay."

"I love you, Celine," she says.

"I love you, too." Before she's even out of the room I'm unconscious.

* * *

I get up at nine the next morning, imagining my classmates in school, looking forward to lunch and laughing away their tedious classes. I feel so removed from them, like the day before at school. Laughing seems impossible. My tears have replenished themselves.

We leave after a quick breakfast. Appropriately, it is pouring, and I shield myself in my mother's arms.

We enter quietly and meet up with Naomi's family again. Today, Dan is stony-faced, avoiding everyone's eyes, like his father. I can't help it; I hug Dan tightly, and awkwardly, he pats my back. I step back and blush.

"It's okay," he mumbles – the only thing he says all day. He touches my shoulder lightly, uncomfortable.

With that, we enter the church and sit in the first row. I catch sight of one of my mother's good friends, here for moral support, and I get a strange look from an unfamiliar woman with bleached-blond curls and huge sunglasses, sitting all alone, before being distracted by my mother's tears.

Alexi takes a seat next to me. Her lips tremble. I squeeze her small, second-grade hand and stay silent, knowing that sisterhood is better than words.

The church fills quickly. My mother keeps turning around to see everyone. The next time I look for her, the woman with the sunglasses is gone, or hidden from view.

The priest begins with an unfamiliar prayer. I bow my head and close my eyes, Naomi's smiling, healthy face swimming beneath my eyelids.

The whole funeral is a blur – only bits stand out to me. Alexi gets up and reads, in her small voice, a poem she personalized last night. Dan's shoulders shake as Alexi reads. The image is heartbreaking, yet also sacred.

Alexi comes down sobbing. I open my arms, squeezing her little body tightly to my own for what feels like hours. She can't stop crying, her shoulders shaking and her face blotchy, but she thanks me and wipes her tears.

I stand up at the end, as everyone begins to file out. I take my guitar from its case and begin strumming. Clara sits at the piano, and at once, we fill the church with sound.

*Amazing Grace, how sweet the sound,*
*That saved a wretch like me...*

People stop and listen, their heads cocked, their eyes shut against tears. I've cried so much today that it seems so natural for my voice to break in the middle of a word. I continue, my eyes streaming and my fingers moving automatically.

All at once the world is silent again, the song complete. My mother is slumped in her seat, her face hidden in my father's broad shoulder.

I see the woman with sunglasses once more, but I can't bring myself to care that she is going up to my parents, lightly tapping my father on the shoulder.

"I'm so sorry for your loss. I'm..." she trails off, and my mother looks up, startled.

The woman takes her sunglasses off and clears her throat. "I'm Sara."

My mother sniffs loudly and, instead of answering, hiccups and then begins to bawl again, hiding her face for a second time. My father tightens his grip around my mother's waist and stares at her.

"We know who you are, Sara." His voice is clipped. "How did you know Naomi was... gone?"

"The newspaper," she says, scuffing her shiny black high-heel against the floor. "I always read the obituaries."

Alexi runs up to me. I hug her, watching the scene as though I'm not a huge part of all of this – as if I'm only a spectator.

"Look, Paul. I'm so very sorry for leaving – you have *no* idea. I missed you, Alyssa, Naomi, the kids..."

"This isn't the time, Sara. I don't know what you expected when you came here." My father stands and half-carries my mother away.

Alexi and I move to follow, but Aunt Sara stops us. "Girls. Oh, my God, *Celine*. You're *so* old. When did you grow up?"

"I guess when you were gone," I say shortly. It's rude of me, but I can't help it. *... And I feel betrayed.*

Sara begins to cry, her clear, white face crumpling and reddening. "CeCe, oh, my little niece... I'm so sorry... you have no idea... I thought about you every day, how sad I was to leave you..."

"Celine – Celine, who is that?" Alexi asks, her little face troubled.

"Why did you come here?" I ask Sara.

"I couldn't help it. Naomi was like my sister, and... God, she *was* my sister." Sara wipes her eyes. "I don't know why I left. Being back here is like *paradise*," she says bitterly, sniffling.

Alexi steps away from me and grasps Aunt Sara's hand. "Don't cry."

"You must be Alexi, all grown up. Eight? Nine?"

"Eight," she answers, staring at our aunt unashamedly. "Second grade."

"God. I wasn't even there for your birth."

I sigh and say, "We have to go. I... I guess you can come with us." I see Alexi's face light up, and know I've made the right decision – at least for now.

We leave, a strange threesome, into the grayness of the outside weather. The rain chills me. I find our car quickly, hurrying inside. Aunt Sara kisses Alexi's hand tenderly.

"I'll see you." Sara says, bidding us goodbye before walking to her car. I see her wipe her eyes covertly.

The casket is raised into a hearse. We drive slowly behind, weaving through streets as we pass Naomi's house. My mother starts to cry again. Neither of my parents has said anything about Sara, but now my father says, "I don't think your mother and I can forgive your aunt."

"Naomi would have," Alexi pleads. She's taken a liking to this phantom aunt of ours.

"Well, it's too late for that now, isn't it?" my mother says spitefully.

"She says she's sorry! And besides, we can't hate just 'cause we've lost Aunt Naomi," Alexi says wisely. "It's called *forgiveness.*"

I stay silent, staring out the window, imagining Naomi walking up and down the block to get customers for our lemonade stands; remembering her inviting grin as she'd stand in the doorway.

I hear my mother say, "Well, it's not that easy, Alexi."

"Why is giving her a second chance so hard? She's your *sister*!" Alexi thinks sisterhood beats all. I can't decide if that's true or not.

"Some sister!" Mom says. "Anyway, even if I forgive her, how will I know she won't run away again?"

"Why did she leave, anyway?" I ask quietly.

"It's... I don't know. It's complicated." Mom leaves it at that.

We pull up to the cemetery. Aunt Sara waits outside for us in the bitter cold. Alexi goes up to her and starts to talk, chattering in her little-girl way, but my mother interrupts; my father and I follow.

"Nice of you to come back," Mom says. Her voice is sharp, like it could actually cut someone.

"Life was stifling me here. You know how I felt about Mom and Dad. I *had* to get out. I just couldn't live with them one more second."

"You could have written!"

"When you were already so angry with me? No, thank you."

My mother groans loudly. "It's not my fault you ran away like that." She turns to us. "Your aunt, here, broke all of my parent's dreams for her – college, a solid job, getting married in a big, white wedding." She looks at Sara disdainfully. "What have you been doing with yourself, anyway?"

"I have a boyfriend, for one thing, who will follow me anywhere. I have a job, and I was just transferred... here."

"Well, don't expect to live in my house! I don't want you running away." My mother's voice is biting, sarcastic.

"You never told me!" I interrupt, unable to help it. "Mom, you never told me *anything* about Aunt Sara! I don't know about Grandpa and Grandma's feelings. *Nothing*. Why am I in the dark about this?"

"Alexi didn't know who I was," Sara says with a break in her voice. "You didn't show them any pictures or tell any stories?"

"Whenever you were in a story, she'd change your name to 'my friend Gretchen' and pretend you didn't exist," I explain. "It took me years to realize there *is* no Gretchen. Only you. And in pictures, she'd never tell us who you were." My voice is reproachful, which I am sorry about, because I really don't want to hurt my mother further.

"I had to protect them!" Mom exclaims. "What was I supposed to say, Sara? 'This is my sister, why ran away like a fool, and now we never speak'? That would have gone over well with little girls! Which *you* wouldn't know, because you always *were* the little girl! Still act like it, anyway."

Sara is crying, but she says defiantly, "You should have told them."

My mother throws her hands up in exasperation. "*You* tell them, Sara. Now that you're back."

My father looks questioningly at my mother. She gives him one look, and he seems to understand. Alexi and I call it *parental communication*, but there is no giggling now.

"I'm not forgiving you. I'm letting you see my children," my mother clarifies. "And maybe, with time, we can have a relationship again, too."

I hear the crushed hope in my mother's voice, and it breaks my heart a little. "Mom..." I say quietly.

"What?" she half-snaps.

"You're my hero."

That does it. She's crying again.

* * *

We go into a tiny room, freezing, and Dan reads a poem, sobbing through it so it's nearly impossible to hear, but a blessing all the same. He looks up and catches my eye, and I channel all of my commending thoughts, my admiration for him and his mother, and my affection for both of them into my look. He gives me a tiny little half-smile, the only time he's smiled in weeks, and it warms my heart to see it. I smile back, and then someone begins to pick up the casket.

Clara's ring accidentally grazes the top, leaving a scratch mark that she stares at in horror. But then someone else leans forward and, using her own ring, carves a heart into the wood. That sets the ball rolling – a woman with a ring on every finger passes them out, and someone else has a Swiss army knife in his pocket. When we are all finished the casket is covered in our little love notes.

I put a big heart, and then a lyric I remember from my song: *sweetest woman*. It is all that fits in the space I've provided myself, but it seems perfect. Dan writes *Mom+Dad 4ever*, and my mother puts *I (heart)*

*U.* Someone writes *amazing grace*, and someone else puts a smiling sun. I'm sure the cemetery workers have never seen anything like this, and I take pride in that.

We leave soon after, tired and hungry, and head to a little party that Clara and my father organized.

When we get into the car, my mother squeezes Aunt Sara's hand, and Alexi plops down on the seat next to her.

That's when I know when everything will be okay.

*Lily Elderkin is an eighth-grader living in a suburb of Chicago, Illinois with her parents and five siblings. Besides writing, she loves to sing and, of course, read!*

# Through Open Eyes

*by Anna Geare*

Those with talent forced to live on the street
As idiot celebrities are living it sweet

Children whose lives are stolen away
Forced into labor for less than a dollar a day

Starvation plagues the world all around
While those with obesity are easily found

Mom 'n' Pop businesses forced out of their shop
While corruption climbs its way to the top

Teens shooting up schools and cutting their wrists
Problems like these just shouldn't exist

Kids replacing a teddy bear with a gun
Addicted to drugs with nowhere to run

Terrorists crashing planes for what they believe
Taking thousands of lives while all others grieve

Energy and resources wasted each and every day
But this problem of Climate Change will not go away

If we want to save this world that we live in
An end to this ignorance really needs to begin

*Anna Geare is seventeen years old and attends Foothill Technology High School in Ventura, California. She has enjoyed writing poems since seventh grade and stage plays since ninth grade. She also spends her free time in her school's robotics club as well as taking acting classes and attending plays.*

# Letting Go

*by Jana Gifford*

So still,
Silent
Like the dead, cold leaves
In Autumn.
Wasted –
Life
Is precious
To the beholder.
But
All things go to the ground
To be lost and
Forgotten
In the shivering, waiting silence.
In the deadness of winter
While the world sleeps and
Cries,
Let us hope.
For hope,

Like tiny seeds,
Finds strength in stillness
And in the deadness
Hears its voice.
The world must wait
And wait it shall
Because it knows that
Hope
Is the greatest growth of all.

*Jana Gifford is an award-winning writer with her debut children's book <u>Of Cabbages and Kings or The Letters of Abby Prince</u> coming soon from The Place in The Woods Publishing. Connect with her at www. janagifford.blogspot.com.*

# Unmask

*by Jana Gifford*

I tilted my mask
a little
to the right
to allow a kindness
in the form of a deed
to escape
but
the effort took both hands
and I found
my mask was slipping off
the love that then flowed
(freely)
brought
such a pleasant sensation
that I stayed unmasked
and so discovered that giving is
truly
receiving

*Jana Gifford is an award-winning writer with her debut children's book <u>Of Cabbages and Kings or The Letters of Abby Prince</u> coming soon from The Place in The Woods Publishing. Connect with her at www. janagifford.blogspot.com.*

# Victory

*by Ioana Grosu*

She carefully balanced her Styrofoam tray on a stack of math books, eager to get out of line as soon as she could. Other students, waiting for their friends, squeezed in on all sides, as if attempting to block her much-wanted exit. Eventually, after much shoving, she made it through into her unnaturally painted blue-and-orange destination: the cafeteria.

There, the hunt began. Her own group of friends was still caught back in the chaos of the line, so it was up to her to snatch an empty table for them. It was a monotonous process, done every day. In a way, being the winner (the first of her friends to make it out of the line) made her the loser (the one who had to find a table).

Ah! There it was! A table waited in front of her, mostly empty, except for a quiet boy from history class. She brushed back her red hair and approached her target. The boy looked up only upon hearing the tell-tale screech of chair leg upon linoleum floor. Confusion flashed in his eyes, but he quickly averted his gaze downwards, back towards the nearly inedible food that was settled neatly upon his own Styrofoam tray.

She smiled at her small victory. Soon, the table would be hers, once her friends managed to escape the line. Her emerald eyes trailed along the faux-wood surface of the table, reading the scratched inscriptions of students past. *Tori loves Jerry. Cammy was here.* They were students like her, with victories similar to hers. The names were just names. But the people who held those titles – Tori, Jerry, Cammy... they all took control of the very same table that she was plotting to conquer.

The boy across from her dared another hesitant glance upwards. He wanted to say something to his momentary companion, but the widely accepted hierarchy implanted in his mind kept him from speaking. He concentrated on other things instead – the incessant jabbering of students, the vigilance of the teachers in charge of them, the sickening smell of what the cafeteria cooks referred to as "food."

He took a bite of pizza and it felt strange in his mouth. It was disgustingly greasy, and residue of wet flour stuck to the bottom. But it was his only sustenance for the next few hours, so he forced himself to chew and swallow. Again and again, he repeated the process, until there was nothing left on his tray to distract him from his unexpected visitor.

The red-haired girl tapped her fingers impatiently on the table, waiting for her friends. When she saw that they would arrive soon, she relaxed, and looked over at her unwanted companion. He was frowning at his empty tray, and she marveled at his courage to actually EAT the food. He looked up at her, and his brown eyes momentarily locked with her own. For different reasons, they broke the gaze, and each went to their own tasks. The girl wondered why he was still there, even though, quite evidently, he had no more food left to eat.

More chairs screeched, and she felt a wave of relief. Her friends were there, signaling her complete conquest of the table. In her happiness, she began to talk excitedly to the other girls. Soon, she forgot about her previous companion, barely noticing when the quiet, brown-haired boy slipped away.

*Ioana Grosu is a freshman at the International Academy East in Troy, Michigan. Her works have been published in The Writer's Slate and Questions: Philosophy for Young People, as well as in several poetry anthologies.*

# I Live In Song

*by Sidney Hirschman*

I live in song
Where I dance
Where I sing
Music flows into me
And is ever-present.
I cannot
Will not
Be any other way
The world may go on
But I live in song.
Where the birds chirp melodies like singers
So familiar
Where the rhythmic winds stir through the trees
That rustle like a pair of maracas
Where the rivers rush and crash
Like dancers stamping their feet.
The work may go on
But I will always
Live in song.

*Edited by Dallas Woodburn*

*Sidney Hirschman lives in Northern California with her family and pets. She enjoys reading, writing, and musical theater. This is her first published work.*

# Feast

*by Victoria Hutchinson*

They sit within the darkness, waiting for the time
to strike.
Hunger gnawing at their innards
They know what lies ahead.
Pawing at the soft ground, they watch the events
unfold:
The demons and angels fight overhead
One after another they fall.
Angels turned malicious and demons all the same
They fight not for honor but for the sake of fighting
untamed.
This roar of battle is tainted not with bravery but
with greed:
The greed of power and the lust of victory fill the
air.
Slowly, the roar lulls into a hush
When all is quiet, they come out for their feast.

Rotting flesh and snapping bones the only noise
now
What a feast, what a feast
Full of feathers not from fowl.

*Victoria Hutchinson is fifteen years old and enjoys writing, drawing, and reading. Her hobby is doll-making. She lives in Cumming, Georgia with her parents. Her brother is a Marine in California.*

# Red Backpack

*by Brooke Jennett*

Why do you tease me, Red Backpack, oh why do you
taunt?
Have I fallen for your color, your zipper, your
pockets,
Your sweetly embossed font?

You want me to leave you –
Leave you right here in peace –
But I can't stop thinking of Red Backpack and me.

We could sit together, in the shade of a tree,
Laughing and happy, Red Backpack and me.

It can't be wrong to want you, oh it can't be wrong
to try,
For without you, Red Backpack, I only want to cry.

It's not just your appearance but what you hide inside,
Because only you, Red Backpack, can go along for the ride.

You can stand out, or stay hidden;
Draw attention, or leave unbidden.

When I cannot find you, Red Backpack, I am scared,
Because me without you is like a legless Fred Astaire.

I love you dearest Red Backpack, and no I don't know why,
Maybe it's that mocking gleam shining in your eye.

Listen to me, Red Backpack, have you any ears?
This is a call of loving, longing, and tears.
For you see, oh Red Backpack, though I love you so,
Someone else carries you, and leaves me here alone.

Go, oh dearest Red Backpack!
But please remember my plea:
Even for a second, could you be carried by me?
I may not be as strong, but I have the largest might,
Oh, red, Red Backpack, could we dance in the night?

This is crazy and I know it, the way I feel for you...
But dearest, dearest Red Backpack,
I hope you know my love is true.

*Brooke Jennett, born in Ventura, California, is now a tenth-grader at Heath High School in Paducah, Kentucky. She is currently working on a novel and is still in love with the boy from her poem.*

# Lápiz

*by Janelle Jewell-Roth*

My tool of destruction and creativity
Building cities with lines of words
Mountains and dragons
Castles and moats
Poems of sadness and ecstasy
New beginnings and painful endings

My utensil of fear and femininity
Constructing characters from life's inspiration
Turning my dreams into reality
Crafting stories from clouds
Moods of depression and awe
Images of beauty and horror
Serial killers and peacemakers

My instrument of paternity and nonsense
Improving the world with words of wonder
Reality and surrealism
Settings of bathrooms and ballrooms
Environments of anger and passion
Auras of calm and chaos
Ferocity and tremulousness

My apparatus of sexuality and shame
Enhancing my writing with ideas
Masochism and spoil-ism
Dreams of arguments and kiss-ups
Personalities springing from doodles
Spirituality and diplomacy

My mechanism of good and evil
Unveiling our morals to show true right from wrong
Procuring alphas and omegas
Illustrating a world seen through a window
Pursuits and journeys
Tremendous losses and beautiful triumphs
Super-villains versus super-heroes

And it all begins with my pencil.

*Janelle Jewell-Roth has been writing for as long as she can remember, poetry in particular. She has written countless poems; "Lápiz" is the first piece she really polished. In eighth grade she won second place at an English Expo with a children's book, and ever since she has been trying harder and harder to finish pieces and submit them to contests or get them published. She is very proud to be part of this anthology.*

# The Ballad For Lady Promise

*by Angela King*

As the bird flies off the branch
As the sand drifts through the sieve
So my faith in Lady Promise
Dwindles to a memory.
Will she leave me to my thoughts?
Can she let me be?
No.
For Lady Promise watches all
Keeping her fingers in the pie
Watching, waiting,
Hoping, praying.
For a chance to come.

Lady Promise left forgotten
Spun to Earth from lofty dreams
Honor, truth have been rejected
Lady Promise is not followed.
Not kept by watchers of the night
Not loved by guardians of the day
So Lady Promise toils for all
And all for nothing.

Critics Business and Prudence claim
That Promise has had her day
Is past the bud of her youth
Has left novelty behind.
Lady Promise, called "old-fashioned"
Gathers dust on an empty shelf:
A tribute gone to shame.

And I?
I worry for my Lady Promise.
I have seen her in her prime
And I have not forgotten
Lady Promise ruled the skies.
As the sun soared
And the moon danced
And the stars smiled benignly
It was she who
Bound lovers together forever
Pulled leaves from green to red
And tied the horizon beneath the
Wings of songbirds.
Lady Promise kept the peace
Lady Promise held Dishonor
And when he squirmed, she silenced him.

Lady Promise, now I beg you,
Do not let our tears run dry!
For as you depart,
We will weep,
And in cold wasteland
Die!

*Angela King wrote this poem in class one day (when she was bored and her teacher was looking the other way). She loves California, rain, books, music, and her very large cat, Zip. She is a Christian.*

# The Things You Say

*by Bethany Krupicka*

Words are mystifying:
One minute they lift you up,
The next, they tear you down,

D

     O

          W

               N,

Down to the ground.
Then up,
Then down.

You are tossed about like a boat in an ocean storm.
A simple "Hello" can build you up.
A harsh "You're no good!" can bring you down.

Words can fly like cannonballs in a war,
And you can't take them back,
So think before you act –
But just the same,
Think before you speak.

*Bethany Krupicka is a fifth-grader from Naperville, Illinois. She loves to play soccer and volleyball. She also volunteers as a costumed interpreter at the living history museum in her city.*

# For The First Time In A Long Time

*by Kienna Kulzer*

I stared out the kitchen window as my hands rinsed the dishes. I used to play out there all the time, but now that my dad is in a wheelchair, there just isn't time. I watched as a scruffy brown dog wandered across the grass. It was a stray that had been around for weeks. I turned off the faucet and ran outside to pet him.

The dog licked my face while I stroked his soft fur. Then he rolled over and I scratched his belly.

"Lizzy?" Dad called as he made his way through the front door. His face lit up in surprise when he saw the dog.

I turned to face him. "Can we keep him? Please?" I begged, running my fingers through the dog's fur.

My dad considered my plea for a minute. Finally, he said, "Oh, all right. It's your reward for being such a trouper."

"Thank you!" I shouted and ran to hug him.

After thanking Dad a thousand times, I led the dog into my room. I sat on my bed and patted the spot next to me. He turned around in a circle before lying down.

"I'll call you… Buttons," I said.

Buttons made a weird face, and then started talking. Really talking. To me.

"Um, hello, Lizzy," he said. "It's great to meet you. Buttons is a good name 'n' all, but would you mind calling me Harvey? That's my real name."

"You… you talk?" I stuttered.

"Well, yes. I can only be heard by people who have experienced extreme hardships. My owner, Samantha, is blind and deaf. She can hear me, too. Why can you hear me?" he asked. I looked down at my feet.

"Sorry," Harvey the dog said. "You don't have to answer that. I was just wondering, that's all."

I took a deep breath and told him about the last few months. I told him about how my best friend, Tiffany, had moved away to the East Coast. Then, just a week later, my parents got into a horrible car accident. A drunk driver ran a red light and smashed into them. The car flipped. I wasn't with them; I was at home with a babysitter. My mom died an hour later in the hospital. Dad broke part of his back and is now in a wheelchair. Now I do almost everything around the house because Dad can't get around very well. He had to quit his job as a construction worker, and now works part-time at a grocery store.

Harvey listened intently the whole time. He even snuggled up against me when I started crying. I always cry when I talk about my mom. I fell asleep with Harvey curled next to me.

We spent the whole weekend together. I took Harvey to the park. We ran around and played Frisbee and tag. For the first time in a long time, I felt like I had a friend. I was really excited when the school secretary phoned saying there'd be no school on Monday because of meetings.

In the middle of the night on Sunday, Harvey woke me. I sat up and rubbed my eyes. "What?" I asked.

He hesitated before answering. "You know how I said my owner was Samantha? Well, it's been really nice here. I love it. But, Lizzy, I really need to get back to her. She needs me. I'm sorry. Really."

"But I need you!" I begged softly, a tear rolling down my cheek. "Please. You're my only friend."

"I need to find Samantha," Harvey said. "Will you help me?"

Even though that was the last thing I wanted to do, I nodded. I felt like it was my duty. To Harvey.

The next day, Harvey and I left my house and walked down the street. "I think I remember how to get there," Harvey said. "But I might need some help."

We'd only walked about half a mile when he stopped in front of a small brick house.

"I don't get it, Harvey," I wondered aloud. "What did you need my help for?"

"I didn't," he replied. "I just wanted you to meet her. C'mon."

Harvey led us to the back door. I opened it. Samantha's room was the first one. She sat up as soon as we walked through the doorway.

"Harvey?" she asked.

"Yes, it's me," he answered. "And I've brought someone with me. Her name is Elizabeth. I think you two will be great friends."

He was right.

*Kienna Kulzer is an eighth-grader at Cabrillo Middle School in Ventura, California. She loves any kind of creative writing, especially short stories and songs. Her other hobbies include hanging out with friends, reading, running, and skiing.*

# My Old Dog

*by Katelyn Larger*

My old dog, Ranger, and I went out into the woods to teach the little pup, Sabine, how to hunt. As we walked through the brush I heard Sabine baying up ahead. Ranger took off after her. When I got there, I saw a huge grizzly bear pushed up against a tree, growling and showing its teeth, with little Sabine howling away in front of it.

The bear lunged straight at Sabine, but Ranger bolted in front of her. The bear sunk its teeth into Ranger's side and started shaking him around.

I shot the bear after finally getting the gun loaded, but I was too late to save Ranger. He was panting and blood was seeping through his copper coat. I started to cry – I couldn't help myself.

"Ranger, it's gonna be all right," I whispered, trying to soothe him. "It will all be over soon."

Looking at him, I knew there was no saving him. I knew what I had to do. I picked up my gun and pointed it at Ranger's torn body.

Everything went black, almost like I was dreaming. I flashed back to the moment I got Ranger.

"You'll make the perfect hunting dog, little guy," I said, putting his dog bed in the back seat of my truck. "Well, what am I gonna name you? Hey, I got it! How about Ranger?"

The pup raised his head and howled in agreement.

Time sped past. My memories flew by, then stopped.

"All right then, Ranger, this is your first real hunt, so make it a good one," I said, encouraging him. I unclipped his leash from his collar and off he went, running like a bullet through the woods with his nose to the ground, ears pricked up, tail wagging. He dashed out of sight for a minute, two minutes. Then I heard him baying. I ducked around an oak tree and saw Ranger, his head to the sky, howling his heart out with a big grizzly bear pinned to a tree. I was so proud of my dog that day.

Then, suddenly, I found myself back in the present: standing in the woods, my gun pointed at Ranger's body.

"I'm so proud of you Ranger," I said, tears rolling down my cheeks. "You're my old dog. The best dog. I won't let you suffer."

He howled a very quiet howl, and then...

... *Bang!*

*Growing up, Katelyn Larger's interests have been playing the clarinet, writing stories, and gardening at her grandmother's greenhouse.*

# Tornado Watch

*by Audrey Larson*

My eyes glazed as I tried to finish my weekend reading assignment. I glanced out my bedroom window, longing to be outdoors. Suddenly, a siren blared through our quiet street. My heart pounded. Was it Saturday or Sunday noontime when they sounded the siren? I couldn't think in my panic. I rushed down the hall of our ranch house to the kitchen. Mom was making lunch.

"It's all right, Wendy," Mom said calmly. "It's just a siren test."

"But Mom, what if there was a real tornado at noon on a Saturday?"

"Worry, worry, worry," Mom said with a smile. "We should call you Worry Wendy."

My parents made two major mistakes in my eleven years:

1. Naming me Windy Daye. (Thank goodness I am now known as Wendy.)

2. Letting me watch the *Wizard of Oz* when I was five years old. This probably has something to do with my tornado phobia. Actually, that's an understatement: I am *petrified* of tornados.

Mom hadn't answered my question. I decided to ask my neighbor, Rachel Jansen. Rachel is a weather fanatic; I bet she'd know.

"Isn't it so cool?" Rachel said, showing me a picture of a gigantic funnel cloud from one of her weather books. Just looking at the picture made my palms sweat.

"Yeah, real cool," I muttered, closing the weather book. "Ever wonder what would happen if a tornado came at the same time as the siren test?"

"Totally unlikely. Anyway, there would be warning beforehand," Rachel said in her know-it-all tone. "Plus, the sky would darken and the siren wouldn't stop."

I felt slightly queasy. I always do after thinking about tornadoes and twisters.

Since kindergarten we had practiced tornado safety in school. I shuddered, imagining the tornado's roar like a train approaching. The instructions played through my mind: *seek shelter in hall on lowest floor, crouch near wall, hands on back of head.*

Rachel sighed. "I'd jump at the chance to see a tornado."

Dorothy's house spinning in the wind came to mind. "You're crazy," I replied.

"Well, as long as it doesn't touch down," she said.

It was springtime, prime tornado season in Harrison, Michigan. When April comes around, I get anxious at every thunderstorm, always on alert.

\* \* \*

A couple weeks later, on a Sunday afternoon, I had the joy of babysitting annoying Maggie Davis from across the street. We were at my house, playing on the swing set in my backyard.

"Hey, Maggs, looks like rain is coming. We'd better go inside."

Four-year-old Maggie shook her head. "I wanna swing!"

"Okay, five more minutes," I sighed.

That's when I noticed a giant gray cloud form. It looked like a thunderstorm.

Then the sky started to darken. "Time's up, Maggie!"

"No!"

A warm wind gusted through the yard. "*Now*, Maggie. There's a storm coming."

A second later my hair was whipping in my face. I grabbed Maggie's hand. "Lets go!"

I looked at the steel-gray sky. Two words flashed through my brain: *Seek shelter.* I ran to the back door and dashed inside. I clicked on the TV.

"I wanna watch Barney!" Maggie cried.

"Ssshh!"

"The National Weather Service has issued a tornado warning..." the newscaster announced. My knees started to shake. "... for the following counties: Franklin, Southfield, and Middlefolk."

Middlefolk County! I took a deep breath. I looked out the window and watched the sky.

"I wanna go home," Maggie pouted.

The grass seemed to shiver as the trees swayed. "Look, Maggie, the trees are dancing."

"I'm scared," she whimpered.

I put my arm around her. The sky was almost black.

The siren sounded.

My mouth went dry. I picked up Maggie and dashed down the basement stairs.

"Let's play copycat, Maggie." I showed her how to bend over with her hands on the back of her head. My heart pounded. "Do what I do."

I heard a rumbling noise. A chill went down my body.

"I want my mommy!" Maggie cried.

"You're safe with me, Maggie. The wind is mad. That's all. We've got to hide so we aren't in its way." I huddled close to her body as the tornado roared.

Then, everything fell silent. My heartbeat drummed in my ears. It was over!

"Come on, Maggie," I said standing up. "Let's see what the wind brought us."

Maggie looked up at me, admiration shining in her eyes. "Okay, Windy."

I smiled. *Windy Daye.* Maybe it wasn't such a bad name after all.

*Audrey Larson lives and homeschools in Sharon, Massachusetts. She is twelve years old and loves to read about history, spies, fantasy and fiction.*

# Fainting in Florida

*by Stephanie Latos*

Have you ever had a sick feeling inside? Have you ever desperately needed to be somewhere else but couldn't move? Have you ever felt trapped in a small space? That happened to me when I was on vacation with my family in Naples, Florida over my 2009 Easter break.

It was Easter Sunday and so we went to Easter Mass at a church near our hotel. Now, Naples has many tourists during this time of year so you can only guess how many people were there...

It was *packed*. I was sandwiched in between a lady I didn't know and my brother. It was *so* hot! I was wearing my nice church outfit and I couldn't stand it any longer. My forehead was so wet that fish could have lived on my face. My hands weren't any better and I had blind spots in my vision. My legs felt wobbly. On top of everything, I needed to use the restroom.

"Mom, where's the restroom?" I asked.

"I'm not sure," she said. "I think it's around that corner in the back of the church."

"Okay." As I squeezed through the row of people, all I could think was, *Gotta get to the restroom.*

When I finally got there, I realized there was only one stall. There was someone in the stall and another woman was waiting in front of me. To make matters worse, someone had gotten sick in the one-and-only sink.

I was losing my vision. All I could see were large colorful splotches. Then my body felt extremely heavy. My legs couldn't support me any longer. I quietly drifted away from consciousness...

"WAKE UP! PUH-LEEEZE WAKE UP!"

I was being shaken by a lady in a yellow sundress with a matching hat. She was crying and her mascara was following her tears all the way down her face.

"Does this happen to you often? Are you all right, my dear?!"

"Yeah, I'm fine. I just need to use the restroom. I'm sorry." My head felt like it was being sandwiched between two forty-pound weights. I finally used the restroom and felt better.

I thanked the lady, left the restroom, and found my parents in our pew. They told me to go up and get Communion, but I knew I wouldn't be able to make it past the first step. Instead of following their directions, I went straight to my seat in our pew. I was about to tell them what happened, but my rescuer came up. She had stopped crying and must have wiped away her smeared mascara.

"You daughter just fainted and I caught her after she collapsed. If there's anything I can do… "

I insisted I was okay, and thanked her for helping me.

Of course my fainting was an epic event in my life, but I hope it doesn't happen to you! Here are some tips to stay on your own two feet:

- Eat a good breakfast.
- Don't force yourself to stay in a stuffy, cramped area.
- Take someone with you if you feel sick.

*Stephanie Latos is a seventh-grade student from Warren, Michigan. In addition to writing, she enjoys running, playing the piano, and playing tennis.*

# The Mystery Of The Stolen Ring

## *by Kay Jin Lee*

It was a rainy night and Ms. Melody was getting ready for her concert. She was to be the solo soprano.

"Milady, your car is waiting," mumbled a smartly dressed butler named Silas.

"Don't mumble, you idiot," snapped Ms. Melody irritably. "And yes, I know that the car is waiting."

Carrying an umbrella in one hand, Ms. Melody stepped out of the door and into the garden. She stopped before the car to pat her two dripping wet, stinky pet Dobermans.

"Boy, do you two stink!" she exclaimed.

"Milady, you are going to get soaking wet if you do not hurry up," said Jackie the chauffeur.

"Then let's go!" retorted Ms. Melody, giving Jackie an icy cold glare that sent chills down his spine.

She stepped into the car and Jackie closed the door behind her.

They arrived at the concert hall to find that they had missed it. Ms. Melody naturally put the blame on her chauffeur.

"You moron!" she bellowed with her world-famous vocals. "You blithering idiot! Why didn't you tell me that it was earlier?"

Jackie rolled his eyes as he drove back to the mansion. How could he have known what time the concert was? Ms. Melody just told him he had to drive here or there. Ms. Melody never told him much.

Ms. Melody stormed into her mansion, fuming. She fumbled with the lock on her room, strode in and slammed the door.

"She seems pretty angry," whispered Bunny, the maid, to the janitor, Bugs.

A moment later the stillness of the night was broken by an ear-piercing shriek.

"Quick! Call the police!" shouted Ms. Melody as she burst from her room, arms flailing like a many-armed octopus. "Call the police!"

Bugs calmed her down while Bunny called the police. Two minutes later, Detective Daff E. Ducke was sent to investigate. He and Ms. Melody went into the dining room and locked the door.

"My name is Detective Daff E. Ducke, and I'm here to investigate," he said, formally introducing himself to Ms. Melody. "Now, what seems to be the matter? The person on the phone just said something terrible happened, so I came to investigate."

Ms. Melody gulped nervously; she had never spoken to a policeman before. "Well," she began, "I was going to a concert and I arrived to find that

I was late. Then, when I came back to my mansion and went into my bedroom..." She trailed off.

"Yes?" prompted Detective Ducke.

"I found that my diamond ring was missing! I had hidden it somewhere and when I came back it was gone. Disappeared!"

"Okay," said Detective Ducke. "So where was it hidden?"

"In a secret compartment under my desk," Ms. Melody replied.

"I shall investigate immediately," said Detective Ducke.

He strode out the door to the scene of the crime. The bedroom was well-furnished with a four-poster bed, a closet and a study desk. There was also a chandelier and a small window. The floor, like the rest of the house, was carpeted.

Perhaps the carpet held a clue: it was wet and stained with mud. There were also some makeshift lock picks on the floor.

Detective Ducke checked under the desk and found the hidden compartment that Ms. Melody had described. He opened it and, sure enough, the ring was nowhere to be found.

He exited the room and requested to see the three people who were in the mansion at the time of the crime. He first brought Bunny into a room and questioned her.

"A burglary has taken place and you are one of the three potential suspects. I am going to ask you a series of questions. Now – "

"Please, I'm innocent. I didn't steal the ring," pleaded Bunny.

"Okay, what were you doing when Ms. Melody was out?" asked Detective Ducke.

"I was tidying up one of the guest rooms."

"Do you possess any special talents?"

"Hmm... You could say I am a pretty good gymnast," Bunny said.

"Did you notice anything out of the ordinary?"

"Yes, Bugs hadn't done his usual duties of cleaning the kitchen."

"Okay, you may leave. But stay in the next room and send Bugs in here."

Bugs knocked on the door and came in.

"Mr. Bugs, a burglary has taken place and I am going to ask a few questions. Now what were you doing when Ms. Melody was out?" questioned Detective Ducke.

"Oh, I was cleaning the windows in the hall," replied Bugs.

"Do you have any, say, special talents?"

"No, not really."

"I understand you hold the keys to Mrs. Melody's bedroom?"

"Yes."

"Did you notice anything suspicious?"

"No."

"Very well," said Detective Ducke. "Please tell the cook I'd like to have a word with him."

The cook opened the door and came in.

Detective Ducke said, "A crime has been committed on this premises and – "

"Was it a murder?" asked the cook, shocked.

"No, it was a burglary. So what were you doing when Ms. Melody was out?"

"I was preparing dinner."

"Do you have any unique talents of any kind?"

"Well, I pride myself on being a master at picking locks," said the cook.

"Did you notice any strange happenings?"

"Yes, Bugs hadn't performed his usual duties of cleaning the kitchen before I went there to cook dinner."

"Fine. That is all I need to know."

Detective Ducke called the other suspects and Ms. Melody back into the room.

"Ladies and Gentlemen," he said to the victim and suspects assembled there. "I know who the culprit is."

"Who is it?" asked Ms. Melody, curious.

"All of the suspects had a reason to dislike Ms. Melody for her rude and unkind behavior," said Detective Ducke. "But the culprit is..." He took a sharp intake of breath and looked at each suspect. Finally, he announced: "Bunny."

"Where's your proof?" asked Bunny defiantly.

"You have every right to ask," said Detective Ducke. "The first thing I noticed was that there was a window. I suspected it to be the point of entry. My suspicions were confirmed when I noticed the carpet was wet and muddy. Also, I only told you there had been a burglary – but you, Bunny, knew that the stolen object was the ring. I'm assuming you scattered some makeshift lock picks to throw me off the scent."

Bunny knew the game was up. She threw the ring into a far corner and yelled, "Catch!" in a high-pitched shriek, and then leapt out the window and made a run for it. Detective Ducke chased out after her. The occupants of the house heard muffled sounds of growling and screaming.

Minutes later, Detective Ducke returned. "We don't have to worry about Bunny committing another crime," he said.

"Where is she?" asked Ms. Melody.

"I'm afraid your dogs were faster than I was," said Detective Ducke.

Two days later, Detective Ducke got a promotion.

*Kay Jin Lee is a grade-six student in the gifted program at Nanyang Primary School in Singapore. When he hasn't got his nose in a book, he enjoys playing competitive tennis and building Lego models. He lives in Singapore with his parents, two older brothers, and a golden retriever.*

# Just One Day

*by Danielle Lemmons*

LilyAnn's broom lifts and falls across the splintered wooden floor.

"Why can't I be out there with other people and have a normal life?" She speaks softly to herself to guarantee that her stern family won't hear.

"It's all because I'm Irish! My horrid background keeps me locked up in this beaten-down apartment like a rat in the alleys of my poor New York."

*Swish. Swish.*

Her broom is the only sound that echoes through the thin walls of the complex. LilyAnn gracefully moves as a sneeze arises in her chest. *ACHU!*

Her head lifts to see her reflection: a pale, rosy-cheeked girl with red, curly locks. Short and thin, just like her mother had been at her age. Green eyes with a speck of gold.

Passing the window, she catches a glimpse of her father swiftly walking towards the apartment.

LilyAnn hurriedly continues to sweep. A newspaper falls from the table as she passes by. Leaning down to pick it up, her eyes are drawn to the date: April 4, 1861.

"Has it really been two years since the move?" she asks herself.

A rapping knock shakes the old, broken door.

LilyAnn runs to the door and peers out the peephole, only to be disappointed.

Willard JoHanson.

A growl rises in the pit of her stomach at the sight of the doughnut-shaped man. His ice-blue eyes are piercing, which startles her. His jet-black bangs only draw attention to those eyes of the killer.

Making JoHanson all the meaner-looking: his missing arm. She heard it was blown off in the Mexican-American War. Summoning her courage, she opens the door and greets him politely.

"Good day, Mr. JoHanson."

"Ha! A good day for you? I imagine not, in this pile of trash you call home."

"Well, I'm sorry you feel that way, Mr. JoHanson, but I've become quite fond of it." Both he and she know it is all her family can afford.

"Look, you little exile, I'm here to collect your rent. Just hand it over and I'll be on my way. Where's your mother?"

"Sir, I'd appreciate it if you didn't call me an exile and –"

"I'll call you what I want, you little rat. Now where's your mother?"

"If you'd let me finish, I'd tell you. She's at the market and won't be in until later. We can only pay you half the rent. The rest of our money has gone to the cause of my father's injury and my burn."

At that, Mr. JoHanson does something no one would expect anyone to do. He grabs LilyAnn's arm where the bandage covers the burned scar from a stove accident. A tear trickles down LilyAnn's poor cheeks as the pain sears through her tiny body.

"AH! Stop, Mr. JoHanson! You're hurting me!" she cries. Her father comes running to the door.

"How dare you touch my daughter! Let her go immediately or I'll – " Before he can finish, Mr. JoHanson further twists the injury, causing LilyAnn to cry out in agony.

"Or you'll what? Come any closer and I will hurt her worse. Your little brat decided to talk back to me and this is her punishment. All I want is my money. If I don't have it by Sunday, I will throw you and your family out on the streets! Is that understood?"

"Yes, sir. My wife and I will have your money. Now please let my daughter go."

Mr. JoHanson drops LilyAnn and walks out the door.

"Thank you, Daddy. I couldn't stop him. I didn't do anything bad. Oh, Daddy, I'm sorry, please forgive me. Are we really going to have to move now? Do we have the money?"

"Hush child. We'll figure it all out. Just lay here and I'll go get some ice for your arm and a cool, wet rag for your face."

"Thank you."

He nods slightly.

"Ugh," LilyAnn sighs to herself. "That crazy man really hurt me. It even looked like he was enjoying it! He's the most horrible man I've ever come across in my life. One day I'll be more powerful than him. Then I'll show him who the boss is. I'll own every building and make sure he gets his payback."

She swiftly runs to her room and flops down on the bed.

"Just one day," she whispers as she drifts to sleep, forgetting the whole world around her.

*Danielle Lemmons is sixteen years old. She has been writing since she was about twelve and has always been inspired by her surroundings. She believes writing is a passion that everyone can benefit from.*

# Aidan's Rage

## *by Naomi Li*

In a time when the world was young, the new Mother Earth raised her youthful features to the strong face of Father Sky. Father Sky fell in love with the beautiful Mother Earth, and he wedded her. In the land where Sky and Earth touched, a great palace appeared. It was made of gold and seemed to pierce the very Sky itself. Fountains spewed water crystal clear. When Diana, the sister of Father Sky, dragged her black, star-sprinkled cloak over the Earth, Mother Earth and Father Sky resumed their human forms: Mother Earth with light green skin and flowing hair; Father Sky a strong man with a beard. At night, the two blissfully enjoyed their great love, till Cyrus, brother of Sky, resumed his form as the Sun and called the two back to their duties.

After several thousand years, Mother Earth and Father Sky were blessed with three children. The first was named Nessa, a pale girl with golden hair and a white silken cloak. In fall, Nessa blew leaves from the trees, her hair entwined with leaves of red, purple, and gold. In winter, Nessa and Father Sky cooperated together to drape snow over hills and mountains. Nessa was a quiet soul, like the snow she made fall over mountains and hills. The winds carried her laughs and sighs. Nessa was winter and fall.

The second child was named Estra, a spirited, slender young girl who had inherited her mother's green skin. Estra coaxed flowers from their icy sleep. She laughed, and the hibernating spring burbled with lively cheer. Nessa went back to her parents' home, and watched the world come to life. Mother Earth, who had become quite cold from all the snow, soaked in Estra's warmth. Estra, being spring and summer, was lively and cheerful, brimming with spirit and curiosity all the time.

Mother Earth and Father Sky had one more child, Aidan. Aidan was the fire that blazed in spring and summer, and cooled in winter and fall. Unfortunately, Aidan's temperament was as fiery as his ability. When Aidan's blood ran high, scorched grass and melted ice was left behind him. This not only deeply upset his sisters, but Aidan's parents also worried. Aidan's flames scorched Mother Earth, and she shuddered in agony. Father Sky coughed long and hard as smoke drifted up to the clouds.

Aidan was repentant; thankfully, his outbursts were rare. But alas, this could not last, for Murrikh, an old enemy of Mother Earth and Father Sky, had found the palace of Sky and Earth.

Murrikh was the god of death and destruction. Long ago, when Murrikh had been a mortal, his greed for power made him a king. Murrikh was cruel, and Mother Earth was disgusted. When he scorned her, Mother Earth shed her old beggar guise and distorted his body. Father Sky put an eternal curse on the arrogant king, taking away his human form. Murrikh responded by bringing death to others. He filled men's heads with bitter rage, pitting them against one another. He stole away the lives of millions.

But what Murrikh wanted most of all was vengeance on Mother Earth and Father Sky; Sky because of the curse he gave him, and Earth for ruining his body. As Murrikh watched Aidan rage, he knew at long last how to avenge himself.

Aidan was sitting on the edge of one of his mother's crystal fountains. His head was bowed, but the flame in his eyes burned brightly. Murrikh swooped down next to Aidan.

"What is it?" asked Murrikh.

Aidan glanced up in alarm, and stared at Murrikh. "Who are you?"

Murrikh laughed, his voice like a serpent slithering over wet rock. The sound was slippery and slick, with a touch of venom inside. "Me?" he hissed softly, "Why, I am a friend."

Murrikh put out a cold pale hand, and his touch filled Aidan's head with anger and resentment, the anger that he used to drive mortal men to their deaths.

"Tell me," whispered Murrikh, "What troubles you?"

When Aidan spoke, his voice was bitter and troubled, as if he wasn't sure that he should be telling the man his feelings, but this half-formed creature would understand how he felt. "It's the girls," he whispered, fearing that Murrikh would scream if he spoke too loud. "They were teasing me, calling me a slowpoke."

In truth, the girls had simply laughed and said that Aidan would have to run faster if he wanted to tag them, but Murrikh had filled Aidan's head with angry thoughts of nonsense.

"Well, do what you like, I'll leave now," said Murrikh, glancing nervously at the advancing Mother Earth. "My home is calling for some tidying up."

Then, with a hiss of air, Murrikh was gone, a black cloud floating away in the darkening sky. Mother Earth came over to Aidan, but he turned away from her. Mother Earth tried to comfort him, but Aidan recoiled from her hand as if it were a spider. Mother Earth, puzzled, went to Father Sky, and they kept a close watch on Aidan, for they had seen the darkness in his eyes.

Winter turned to spring. Laughing, Nessa happily journeyed home. Aidan, maddened with rage and unreason, struck out at her, believing that she laughed to hurt him. Nessa was caught by surprise, and she was quickly melted to a puddle. Soon she was but a droplet of water. Aidan, however, had no remorse. He was going to kill the seasons, until only fire remained for mortals, scorching them day and night.

Tumbling helplessly from the sky was Nessa, a miniscule little girl made of water. By good fortune, she landed on an aspen tree leaf. Ilan, the tree god, quickly spirited her back to the palace, where Nessa stayed, frightened and terrified.

Estra flew on spring green wings, awakening an old maple, creating a young ash sapling. She woke the old spring, singing sweet songs in its ear. Cheeks flushed, Estra flew on, covering the Earth in a grassy carpet.

Laughing, Estra flew on to a sleeping volcano. Her laughter paused abruptly. Frowning, Estra tried again to cover the volcano with grass, but to no avail. Estra dove into the volcano.

Inside the sleeping giant, a small dark form was huddled on a stub of rock. Estra took a closer look, and laughed at Aidan's sulky form.

"Come, brother!" she chirruped playfully. "Don't brood around in this big old dragon."

Aidan raised his head furiously. Estra saw the burning fury in his eyes and fled for her life. She leapt over a groaning peach tree just as Aidan emitted a birdlike shriek and assumed the form of a firebird, with burning eyes glowing with fury, and wings of molten lava. He spat out coals of flame, which joined into a gigantic fireball. Furious, Aidan set out to kill.

Estra screamed in terror, and assumed a form of her own, the squirrel. Swift and agile, she leapt from branch to branch as Aidan's fury destroyed her paradise. Estra sobbed uncontrollably as her brother bore down upon her, trapped and helpless in a corner, and smote her ruthlessly.

Aidan reassumed his form as a boy. All of a sudden, he felt terribly small; sweat drenched his floppy brown hair and dripped into his dark brown eyes. He stared at his sister, a tiny pile of burnt leaves. He stared, unable to believe that he had committed murder. His head dropped to his chest. Murrikh had tricked him. He didn't feel satisfied in the least. All Aidan felt was sorrow; a deep sorrow that went from his belly and clawed its way out as an unearthly shriek of repentance, grief, and loss.

As the sound of Aidan's crunching boots faded away, Estra stirred feebly. She blinked, brown eyes full of excruciating pain. A huff sounded behind her, and Estra turned to see a large brown bear. It looked at her carefully. Estra quaked in fear as the great animal advanced upon her. The bear huffed again, and then nuzzled the goddess of spring and summer as tenderly as if she were a newborn cub. Hardly daring to breathe, Estra entwined her fingers in the fur of the great beast. Nudged onto the bear's back, Estra was carried to a cave, where she was enveloped in a blanket of soft darkness.

Estra awoke to the steady stream of something in her mouth. Frail and tiny, she sucked at it faintly. The devastation of the fire had reduced her to a size so small that geese seemed the size of her mother and father. As Estra continued to suck at this delicious something, the young goddess realized that she was drinking milk. Bear's milk. Estra gently pet the mother bear as she fed. When Estra felt full, the bear looked at her with loving eyes. Estra whispered, "Thank you," and slept on.

The days passed. Estra and her new friend frolicked in meadows and laughed. Estra healed, thanked the bear, and left to restore spring. The brown-furred mother watched the girl go, then lumbered back to her den.

Estra flew, gradually gaining altitude as she went. Flying to the sleeping volcano, Estra shot straight into the great giant. Huddled miserably on a rock was Aidan, tears splashing onto the cold earth. Estra hurried over to her brother in concern, and she placed a gentle hand on his shoulder. Aidan started at his sister in wonderment. "Are you alive?" he whispered.

"Yes," said Estra.

Aidan threw himself at his sister's feet. "Oh Estra," he sobbed. "I've done a terrible thing! I've melted Nessa and she'll never come back!"

"Nessa is healing at home," Estra replied gently. "We are all safe. We don't blame you."

The two set out for home, where their family was waiting with love and tenderness. Murrikh never troubled the family again, for he realized in defeat that the power of love was far greater than the influence of anger and death that he brought. All was well as Cyrus rose for a new day of life, to celebrate the undying power that binds a family together: love.

*Naomi Li is a sixth-grader at Southern Lenigh Intermediate School in Pennsylvania. She has two sisters and two wonderful parents who encourage her literary pursuits and spur her on to shoot for the stars.*

# The Fantastic Trip

*by Ninad Mahajan*

Have you ever wanted to know what life is like in India? The climate? The food? The people? Well, today is your lucky day, because I am going to take you on a "remarkable journey" through India!

Seven thousand, two hundred miles. That's how far India is from the United States. And the flight time? Fifteen hours. Yes, I know that's a long time, but I entertained myself with some games on a built-in entertainment system on the back of the airplane seat in front of me! (Cool, right?) When I got off the plane, it was only a few minutes until I saw my grandparents and uncle. They live in Mumbai [Moom•bye], India. We took a car to their house, a place I hadn't seen for five-and-a-half years! After a quick dinner, it was off to bed. I knew tomorrow would be a big day to explore!

The next morning, my grandfather showed me an instrument called a harmonium, which is

127

similar to the piano. The difference is that its keys are colored green and brown instead of white and black. I played some songs I knew on it. It sounded like an accordion. I liked playing this instrument.

After two days, I left Mumbai and went on a three-hour trip to another city in India, Pune [Poo•nay]. My aunt lives there in an apartment. When we arrived, I saw my cousins and thought, "I don't seem to remember my relatives that well." Everybody ate lunch and then I went to sleep because I was very tired. When I woke up, I went to look for my brother and cousins. They were watching TV. I didn't understand anything because it was all in an Indian language called Hindi [Hin•dee]. Later, we went outside to play a game similar to baseball called cricket. We had a great time playing. When it was time to leave, I was sad to say goodbye to my cousins, but I also wondered where we would go next!

We left Pune and headed for another city called Savda [Sow•dah]. It was pitch dark when we arrived because it took ten hours to get there. My cousins were eagerly waiting to meet us. Their house was gigantic! It had two floors, plus a terrace. A terrace is basically a huge sky deck. Also, on the second floor, there were three balconies to see everything that was going on outside.

We stayed at this house for two weeks. As the time passed, I made lots of new friends. They came over to play sports with my brother and me everyday. One day, I took out a game that I had brought from the U.S. and let them play with it. It was similar to the Wii. They loved it, and I was glad because they didn't have many games and toys to use.

During our time in Savda, my mom, brother and I took a trip to the farmland that my grandparents own. I saw cotton, mangoes, papayas, and lots of bananas. I had never seen so much farmland before in my life. My grandma explained to me where our property ended and also what they do with the food and grains they grow. Wow! So much effort goes into growing a simple banana or a mango that we eat at home. When I eat food, I don't usually stop to think about where it came from or the farmer who took care of it so I could enjoy it.

In India, ants come in many sizes. On the ground, I saw ants the size of a raisin. Then we walked some more to see the cows and buffalo. That's where we get our milk. It was so beautiful to see the green grass all around. Everyone was tired, so we sat under a huge mango tree and drank some delicious mango juice. It was very refreshing after a long, tiring day. I will never forget this experience.

It was time to go back to Mumbai, but before I left, I went to see my friends' houses. I couldn't believe it! My friends' houses were so small and didn't have many things, such as computers or video game systems. When we played together all those days, I never thought their lives were like this. Life in India is so hard for some people, yet they are still happy with the few things they do have. Driving away, I peeked out the car window and waved goodbye to the people who taught me a very valuable lesson.

Back to square one: Mumbai, India! We visited a huge mall called CityCenter and played arcade games and went bowling. A bowling game cost sixty rupees [roo•pees], which is only $1.50 in U.S. dollars. (Forty rupees are equal to one U.S. dollar.) I didn't do very well, until I got nine pins on one throw. The pin-setter knocked the other one down, so I got a strike. I yelled "Yes!"

Before going home, we stopped to get some hot Indian food. One of the foods was called a dosa [doh•sah]. It was like a pancake, but made out of rice. I loved the food. I felt like I never wanted to go home!

But all good things must come to an end. It was fun, but I had to return to my normal life. At the airport, I said goodbye to my grandparents and uncle. I walked up to the steps of the plane and sat down in my seat. I looked out the window as the plane took off. And just like that, all I could see of India were little dots.

Home sweet home! I was sad and happy at the same time to be back in the United States. I know that one day I will return to India and maybe visit new places. I can't wait for my next fantastic trip!

*Ninad Mahajan is a fun-loving, bright fifth-grader who enjoys school. He especially loves to read and write. He has blossomed over the past year with his writing.*

# Instructions For The Landscape

*by Juliet McLachlan*

Landscape,
spread this heart of yours
across the plains and hills and lakes.

Put color through the sky,
mold the earth into a ball,
spill your tears for the oceans,
open your wings for the animals,
hang the marine animals over the sea,
sprinkle light onto the world.

Landscape,
put your life in mine.

*Juliet McLachlan is nine years old and is a student at Kirkwood Intermediate in Christchurch, New Zealand. She had two previous poems published in New Zealand in 2009. Writing poetry is an important part of her life.*

# Coming/Going Home

*by Emma Elisabeth McNairy*

My happiest moment occurs every time I come home. You see, I am fifteen and go to boarding school. I love it there, but I am human and get homesick. I need my mum, and yearn for my very own bed and an escape from constant school life. So for me, there is no happier time than coming home.

The moment I see my mum's car drive up to the school is exhilarating; taking the highway exit to go back to my hometown relieving; and collapsing in my perfectly rumpled bed satisfying. However, the best, happiest moment of all is getting a hug from my little sister.

She comes down the steps of the school bus; her backpack, not quite secure on her shoulders, slips from one arm. I itch to straighten it. Finally, firm on the sparse, scratchy grass of our front yard, she pauses to adjust the straps. She resumes walking, then – looks up. When she sees me, though I am just an ordinary person grimy with travel, her grin is gorgeous. Seeing her is better than any moment in a movie, more true than poetry – she is more beautiful, shining, real than the sun. She runs to me, I to her. We hug and I bury my face in her hair, which smells of flowers because she never fully rinses out shampoo.

She has grown; every visit I find her taller than I remembered. Next vacation, I won't be able to tuck her head under my chin when we embrace. Soon, she will knock me over when she runs to me. Sometimes her hair is longer. Other times, she has had it cut, though I have not gone to the hair-cutter with her, reading trashy magazines in the waiting room and then laughing with her about the ridiculous "10 Hottest Beauty Trends!"

Every time I come home something has changed, and I scramble to spot the differences. But these are not thoughts for a first-hug-home, and I put them aside. Instead, I bask in the joy of being with my little sister again. I draw back, noticing how well she fits my old T-shirt, which she must have taken from my closet while I was gone. Part of me wants to stop the change, freeze this moment, so that I will always recognize every inch of my sister, so that none of her will ever be foreign. Yet I am content, delighted that she can be a bit alien, yet still love me; that she is not precisely how I last pictured her, yet I still love her.

She says my name, and her voice – perhaps a bit lower than before – resounds in me as it always has.

*Emma Elisabeth McNairy is a boarding-school student in North Carolina. She enjoys taking walks, listening to NPR, and going to art museums. She likes old films, fountain pens, her family, and writing in the third person about herself.*

# Real

*by Emma Elisabeth McNairy*

I am sitting on the sun porch, doing homework,
calculus and chemistry, manipulating the ideas of
somethings:
variables undefined, atoms invisible,
ideas too small, too vague for my comprehension.
I have whole pages of this, in cramped ballpoint,
the scribbles of in-class notes more symbol than
script,
I fill whole notebooks with things that I secretly
believe do not exist.

The sun sets earlier each night,
(emitting spectacular rays of stunning color
created by vibrating electron nonsense),
so it is dark when at 7:08 pm the public safety man
comes round.

He gives each of the French doors a firm tug,
checking to see that they are securely locked against
invisible threats,
checking to see that we cannot be invaded.
This shadow figure, whose name I do not know,
defends against what is unimaginable and yet
foreseen.

His movements rattle the glass in front of my
sanctuary.
I look up, and we smile at each other, give weak
waves,
to reassure each other, ourselves,
that we are still real, two true human beings,
even as we muddle with the imagined.

*Emma Elisabeth McNairy is a boarding-school student in North Carolina. She enjoys taking walks, listening to NPR, and going to art museums. She likes old films, fountain pens, her family, and writing in the third person about herself.*

# Dancing Through Space

*by Mallory McPherson-Wehan*

Darting stars creep across the night sky,
Behind them rays of internal light spreading into
A million gold handprints.
The midnight sky,
Like a rollercoaster of connecting suns
And pirouetting stars.
I wonder how they became
The specks of firefly that I see now
Luminous against the charcoal sky
Playing tag with the silver suns.
Leaning against the warm ground,
Feeling the pulse of the earth beneath,
I realize that once you see the stars for yourself,
You never see anything the same.

*Mallory McPherson-Wehan is fourteen years old and currently resides in Ventura, California. She has been writing for as long as she can remember and is looking forward to a future of writing.*

# Pegasus And Belleraphon

### *by Mirriam Neal*

Sailing over aqua seas,
Eyes like burning ice.
Feathers white as purity,
No rider will this horse suffice.
Belleraphon! With golden bridle.
Belleraphon! With brazen face.
Belleraphon! Was standing idle
As he waited at the place.

Then lo! Behold, this splendid sight,
The sacred white horse in his flight!
He circles! Full attention he demands,
From his watcher as he lands.
His golden hooves grace the sea of green,
His snowy coat with satin sheen.
The gusts that his mighty wings blast,
Bends the emerald blades of grass.

Belleraphon! He sees it all
Belleraphon! The horse is tall,
But the young man has steely courage
And the sight of the horse does not discourage.
He creeps from his place with brown eyes keen,
Fixed on the steed that is fit for a king.
His muscles coiled like a spring,
His tawny head like a lion's mane.

The Pegasus, he lifts his head,
And catches something on the wind.
His nostrils flare as he prepares for flight.
But just as he begins to lift,
Belleraphon! Crosses the rift.
He leaps onto the white steed's back.
Away they go! Into the air!
They struggle above, this strange pair.

Belleraphon! Though death defying,
Keeps his head and begins bridling.
The winged horse fights and bucks and turns
To escape the golden bridle.
But it the Maker forged with magic,
So that nothing could withstand it.
Belleraphon, with hands of steel,
Holds onto the horse's mane
As the stallion starts to reel.
His wings fold, he starts to spin,
Belleraphon, he sees his life before his eyes
And prays to God to forgive his sin.

But as his hands take hold the reins,
A miracle happens, begins to unfold –
The horse starts flying, smooth as you please,
With no sharp kicks, no bucking knees.
Belleraphon! With face so fair,
Swoops down into the Chimera's lair.
Can he do it? Can he defeat the beast?
With the help of the Pegasus, it is a small feat.

As soon as the land is rid of the horror,
Belleraphon! He lands the mighty horse.
"You may go, creature of the heavens,
I could never keep you without your trust."
He slips the magic bridle off,
The steed's fine head is free again.
His muscles ripple as he gallops away,
Flying off into the rain.
The thunder booms, the lightning cracks
As the Pegasus is gone from there.
Tears mix with rain on the young man's face
As his heart breaks for the horse of the air.

But suddenly, through a flash of light,
He is standing there, a noble sight –
The Pegasus has returned to man.
The flying stallion's large eyes say
"It is only you I've learned to trust,
And without two there is no us.
I have decided with you to stay,
Now come! Come! Let us fly away."

Belleraphon! Leaps onto his back,
As the Pegasus flies to whence he came.
The golden bridle falls to the ground,
No more need of it is there
As long as love shall bind the pair.
No more have either of them been seen,
But they still live somewhere in the air,
Where they both reign supreme.

*Mirriam Neal is a sixteen-year-old Christian girl who loves God, family, and friends. Her favorite activities are writing stories, books and poems; reading; drawing; and listening to a wide variety of music.*

# The Silver Rose

*by Emily Nelson*

Silver petals glistening in the sun
Solid as a stone, cold as the snow
Beautiful in its own way
Sharp and delicate
Wise and silent
You live immortal
Unknowing of light or dark
Rain, shine, or snow
Yet, your petals drip dewy tears
Silver spills on the ground
The wind whistles through you
Creating a sound so pitiful,
So heartbreaking
You'll never be the desired gift
For a lover or a friend
Passed over for the tulips and posies
The commoners, the expected
And you, my sweet, sit here alone

Watching the husbands pass you over
You are exquisite
So very unique
Yet, here you will stay
A pretty decoration in a window display
All because no one will trust
A silver rose with glass thorns.

*Emily Nelson currently attends Ladysmith High School and loves to write and read in her spare time. She hopes to go into a medical profession.*

# Winter

*by Bryce Perea*

Winter is the time
For Jimmy.
He loves to snowboard –
Started when he was three
And now he is fourteen.
His favorite season
Is winter.

One winter day
Jimmy was snowboarding
Down the mountain.
He heard a grumble.
Looked behind him and saw
A wall of snow.

He snowboarded
Down that mountain
For his life.

Finally, he reached the bottom.
Beat the avalanche.
He said,
*Thrill is the reason*
*I love the winter.*

*Bryce Perea is fourteen years old and attends eighth grade at Sidney Middle School in Ohio. He loves playing the drums and bass guitar. He also loves to snowboard.*

# Conscience

## by Rachel Phillips

Hi there.

It's me, your conscience. Betcha never heard that one before, huh? Anyway, I'm speaking on behalf of, well... you. Wait! Don't tell me to shut up just yet! Humor me, please.

Okay. Your entire life, you've been an enormous, walking, talking pair of ears. Let me explain. When you were just a little baby and I was just barely starting to become a part of your life, you listened. You listened to the people around you – the words they spoke and the messages they conveyed with their actions.

But you not only listen, you *mirrored*. You took the messages you heard and responded to them. In some way or another, you started acting and saying similar things. *Well*, you're thinking, *I was a baby then. All babies do that.*

Guess what? Babies aren't the only ones.

As you grew up, you met wonderful people called friends. They, too, were ears and mirrors. You began to mimic them; they, in turn, mimicked you.

You started to see television shows, movies, advertisements, etc. You may like to think the media had no impression on you. But you have been influenced. Everyone has been.

In the course of your entire life, you will meet many more mirrors. The bosses you have, the new friends you meet, the people waiting in line at the store. Everyone.

Isn't it amazing? You've heard it your whole life: *Be proud of yourself, but don't be arrogant. Live up to society's standards of beauty, but don't be superficial. Be smart, but not so smart that you intimidate the opposite sex. Be yourself, but don't be too different from everyone else.*

Wait, what?

It's truly astounding. All humans have heard this and responded. For the most part, few people really question the spoken and unspoken rules that, frankly, don't always make sense.

Now let me ask you a question.

When was the last time you thought for yourself?

Careful, don't answer too quickly. Take time to ponder your response.

And let me tell you something else.

There is hope. You are a human being – by definition, you are unique. Although you take in a never-ending stream of social cues, you are yourself.

You are beautiful. You are flawed. You are absolutely, utterly unique.

Now, don't get me wrong. I'm not saying that you should rebel against everything everyone tells you. Where would you be without some sort of base?

I have a proposal.

Add a pair of eyes to your ears. Really take a long look at your family, your friends, your community, yourself. Carefully weigh all that they have told you. Realize their valid points and their differences. Decide. Who are you and what do you really, truly believe in? What do you stand for?

And then go for it. Do something remarkable: live authentically.

*Rachel Phillips was born in Iowa and moved to Mozambique, Africa for two years. She currently lives in California with her parents, a dog, and two very fat cats. Rachel wants to become an international journalist and eat an unprecedented amount of olives.*

# Unwelcome

### *by Rachel Phillips*

Why, hello, Mr. Cliché! How nice of you to drop by!
My house is your house, you know.
Needless to say, I have the time of'my life
When you and the missus decide to show.
Wait a sec, what's that you say?
You're feeling like a tired old cliché?
Oh, come on, good sir! I beg to differ!
Even if you feel a bit under the weather,
When life gives you lemons, make lemonade
Because every cloud has a silver lining, eh?
And when push comes to shove, practice makes
perfect.
It's a no-brainer, I think. The truth is a far cry
From your half-baked idea that you're not what you
are –
A diamond in the rough!
Why, love is blind do or die see eye to eye pat on the
back pushing up daises spill the beans no cigar all

eyes give and take over the hill hands on spitting image sink or swim pull my leg hard to swallow bottom out hand over fist survival of the fittest all in due time and when it rains it pours!
When all is said and done, Mr. Cliché,
Maybe you *shouldn't* visit anymore.

*Rachel Phillips was born in Iowa and moved to Mozambique, Africa for two years. She currently lives in California with her parents, a dog, and two very fat cats. Rachel wants to become an international journalist and eat an unprecedented amount of olives.*

# i am me

*by rachel phillips*

like a leaf has two sides
veins stretching as fingers
clinging to the branch
so is a name.
such a funny thing – a name is just
a word
a sound
some letters.
but it isn't just
all that.
a name is a path
that you can travel
to find your true self.
it doesn't have to be just
your birth name or
your nickname.
it longs to be more than just
all that.

it is the essence of
your soul
deep within.
your own identity.
it is the reason you can
say i am me
and i am proud.

*Rachel Phillips was born in Iowa and moved to Mozambique, Africa for two years. She currently lives in California with her parents, a dog, and two very fat cats. Rachel wants to become an international journalist and eat an unprecedented amount of olives.*

# The Beach

*by Ivy Pike*

I always like summer
best.
You can eat fresh watermelon
from your garden
and greens
and lots of
fruit
and ice cream
at the beach
and listen to music
outside
in the warm sand
and run all over
barefoot
and feel the warm breeze
blow throw your hair
and stay up
all night long...

*Ivy Pike was born on June 9, 1997. She lives in Ventura, California, and her hobbies include soccer and surfing.*

# Blue

*by Ivy Pike*

A jewel on a king's finger
A newborn baby's eyes
The sound of peace
A tall glass of water
A young girl singing
The taste of sweetness
A cold raindrop falling on your face
The sky free of clouds...
Blue can lift you in a dream.

*Ivy Pike was born on June 9, 1997. She lives in Ventura, California, and her hobbies include soccer and surfing.*

# The Land Of The Violet Blood

*by Kalia Prescott*

He leaned in so close she could feel the warmth of his breath on her cheek.

"But how do I know I can trust you?" Zelia whispered through dark lips that were surrounded by a tear-stained face.

"They don't know what's best for you, Zelia," the boy said. "I know what's best for you. Because I love you."

A tear ran down Zelia's pale cheek, and her mascara smeared under her eyes. *I love you.* Zelia had never heard these words before, much less from a boy she had barely met.

*How can I trust this guy?!* Zelia thought. *He probably just knows how to pull my heartstrings to get me to follow him, so that he can take me to a secret lair and hurt me! But then how does he know all this stuff about my life? He's a stalker! That's why he "loves" me! He's spent so much time around me, without me knowing of course, that he fell in love with me! But then, why would he choose me to follow around?*

Zelia was flustered. The branches of bare trees seemed to trap them in the woods.

The one thing Zelia wanted more than anything was to be away from her selfish family. They wasted their money on drugs. They wasted their lives in crime, drinking, and partying. They considered her a slave, and treated her so. This guy was right. But Zelia was still confused. Sensing her reluctance, he took her hand and led her through the woods.

They walked briskly until they reached a clearing. *I've been through these woods a million times! How could I have not noticed this?* Zelia wondered as a glittering creek shone clear and pure in the clearing. All she could do was gasp at the peaceful, perfect scenery. It felt magical. The boy walked forward, heading slowly towards the creek. Zelia followed, in a trance-like state, captivated by the beautiful violet moon. In fact, the whole sky was violet!

Zelia looked down. The grass was also violet, and the trees, and the creek. Zelia looked at her own hands. They were glowing with a strong white light, just like the rest of her body. The boy turned around and took her hands. He was glowing, too. Zelia's heart began to beat faster. His hands were cool. They sent a tingle down her spine. It felt almost as if little magical needles were pricking her hands.

The boy and Zelia began to lift into the sky, heading straight up, towards the violet moon. Zelia lurched forward and grasped the boy's shoulders with her hands, and her head fell against his chest.

He held onto her as they took off through the sky. The wind stung her cheek. She noticed, for the first time, that a pair of wings had sprung forth from the boy's back. The wings were also violet, and as thin as lace.

Before Zelia knew it, the boy was sprinkling violet dust on her head. "Sleep, my love," he whispered. "You mustn't see the way to my home."

Zelia awoke underground. Deep, deep underground. She sat up, her silky hair curtaining her pale face. The boy knelt next to her, the handsome boy who had brought her to this place.

"Where am I?" Zelia asked. The boy's intense violet eyes made her feel breathless, and his pale skin appeared as light and flawless as clouds.

"My name is Azarr," he said, "and you are in my home."

Zelia sat up and looked around. "Where do you live? And, I saw you, you had, you had…" Zelia didn't want to say "wings." She didn't know if she had actually seen them, or if she had been dreaming.

"I know, I had wings. I still do." Azarr said, turning so his wings were visible to Zelia. She closed her eyes and opened them, but the wings were still there. Zelia felt faint. The next thing she knew, Azarr's strong hands were around her.

"Are you okay?" he said, concern creasing his face.

"Where am I?" Zelia demanded.

"You, my love, are in the land of the Fey. You are in Zelia." The last word seemed to melt off his tongue like hot fudge slides down a sundae. "You must have many questions. Yes, the land of the Fey is called Zelia. That is because you are a reincarnation of Queen Zelia, the woman who was the first ruler of the Fey people. I have been watching you, Zelia. I know that you don't want to be a slave to your parents any longer. I can see the scars on your arms, from when they beat you. I also know that you are Scottish, German, Russian... and Fey. I can see the flecks of violet in your eyes. You are Fey. All you need is a... well, a kiss from another Fey, and you will be one of us. You will rule Zelia, and peace will return to the land."

Zelia wanted to believe him, she really did.

"I believe you," she said hesitantly. "But I barely know you. I'm willing to stay, but I need to know more. I may not want to be Fey."

Azarr leaned in close, so close she could feel the warmth of his breath on her lips. "I will never make you do anything you don't want to. You may barely know me, Zelia, but I know you better than anyone ever will."

*Kalia Prescott loves Tae Kwon Do, riding horses (jumping) and fashion. She especially loves all her best friends: Alyson, Miranda, Harrison, and Natalie. She is so grateful to have her story published, and a big thanks to Write On! Books for making it possible.*

# Happiness On A Waffle Cone

*by Yesenia Quirino*

There is a place I go
when I need something sweet:
The Ice Cream Shop is the place to be.

The smell of the flavors and the waffle cones
to munch down on after there is no more.

The sensation is like no other
when you see all the colors –
they shine like light –
come on and take a bite.

It's happiness
on a waffle cone.

How many scoops?
One? Two?
Three?
Come inside to taste a sweet frozen treat!

Just take a lick
and don't forget
to leave a good tip!

*Yesenia Quirino is an eleven-year-old sixth-grader who lives in Oxnard, California. She has always loved writing poetry and short stories.*

# All Is Well

*by Austin Rogers*

When a baby wails,
the mother whispers into the child's ear,
and all is well.

People laugh on the beach,
the bird flies high into the sky,
and all is well.

A picnic in the park,
people share a silent, blissful moment,
and all is well.

Dancing at a party,
perspiring with joy,
all is well.

Throwing a baseball with your son,
having lots of fun,
all is well.

Cherishing the warmth of the fireplace
on a snowy afternoon,
your world is at peace.

The movers of success dream of happiness for the
world.
Adults work hard to ensure happiness for their
children.
Actors, directors, and producers make movies
to lighten the mood in hard times.

And as this is all happening,
the mother whispers in the child's ear,
and all is well.

*Austin Rogers lives in Ventura, California with his
mother. He enjoys soccer, basketball, and playing
improvisational jazz on his saxophone.*

# Bye, Jonny

*by Josiah Rood*

I ride my bike to 1423 Oak Street to meet up with Jonny. We have been best friends for nearly ten years. When I arrive at Jonny's house he is waiting for me in his driveway as usual, ready to take off. We ride together to school, talking and joking.

The bell rings, and we part ways.

"Bye, Jonny!" I call.

"See ya!" he replies.

I walk down the hall to science class. Today we get to dissect a frog. An "animal activist" sits next to me and she starts crying when I pull out the frog's heart.

Second period, math class, doesn't go much better. "Open your calculus books to chapter five!" Mr. Benton says. "Today we begin studying the anti-derivative!"

I am relieved to meet up with Jonny for study skills class in the library. The teacher makes us sit at separate ends of the room. But that doesn't stop us from having fun.

"Go long!" I yell as I sling a football across the room to Jonny. It crashes into Mrs. Ross, the five-foot-tall, prehistoric Language Arts teacher. Whoops!

"Sorry!" I say. But Jonny and I are dragged to Principal Gunther's office.

"Why were you two throwing a football in the library?" he sighs, closing the door behind us. "You hit poor Mrs. Ross in the face! I should have you both suspended!"

"I-I-I'm sorry," I stutter.

"Me t-t-too," says Jonny.

"Is that all you have to say for yourselves? Now who threw the ball?"

"I-I did, s-s-sir," I manage to spit out.

"Well then, Jonny, you're excused. You may go back to class now."

"But it was my football – it was my fault, too – "

"Go back to class, Jonny!"

"Okay," Jonny says reluctantly, shooting me an apologetic look before closing the door behind him.

"So," Principal Guthrie says, narrowing his eyes at me. "Why did you throw that football at Mrs. Ross?"

"I didn't mean for it to hit her. It was an accident, I swear. We were just having fun."

"Fun! Well, you can have more fun during your two after-school detentions. One tomorrow, one on Friday."

I catch up with Jonny at lunch.

"What happened?" he asks.

"Two days of after-school detention."

"I'm sorry I told you to throw that ball."

"It's all right. I'm glad you didn't get detention, too."

"You're a great friend," Jonny tells me.

"You would have done the same for me," I reply.

"Wanna come over after school?" he asks.

"Sure."

The final bell can't come fast enough. Jonny and I ride our bikes home together. I try to forget about detention.

As night falls, I say goodbye to Jonny and head home for dinner. My sister, Laura, opens our front door.

"Where have you been?" she says.

"I was at Jonny's doing homework. Why?"

"Mom and Dad are out looking for you. They're either really mad or really sad. I can't tell. They said they have something to tell us, but they wanted to wait until you got home."

A few minutes later, our parents get home and corral us into the family room.

"We have something to tell you," Dad says, taking a deep breath. Mom rubs his shoulder. "Mrs. Hobart passed away today."

Mrs. Hobart is an old lady who lives across the street. Her husband died a long time ago. Sometimes her kids and grandkids came to visit her, but usually she was by herself. She used to babysit Laura and me when we were little. She drove a big black pick-up truck and told corny jokes that made my parents laugh, but seemed pretty dumb to me. I'm sad she died, but it feels kind of removed from my life. I didn't know her very well. I can't even remember the last time I saw her.

"The funeral is on Saturday," Mom says.

"Can Jonny come?" I ask. I've never been to a funeral before. The idea of it makes me nervous. I know it'll be better if Jonny's with me.

"I guess that's all right," Mom says. "As long as you boys can behave and be respectful."

"We will. I promise."

We pick Jonny up for the funeral on Saturday morning. He's wearing a black suit and tie. If Laura didn't have a crush on him before, I can tell she does now. She smiles at him and smoothes down her hair with her hand.

The funeral passes by quickly. A few people get up and say nice things about Mrs. Hobart, including Laura, who reads a poem she wrote about birds soaring free. Afterwards we go up to Mrs. Hobart's family and give them our condolences.

"I'm sorry for your loss," Jonny says. I'm surprised to see tears in his eyes.

"Wait, did you know Mrs. Hobart?" I whisper as we walk out of the church.

"No," he says. "But it's a shame. She sounds like a great person." He sighs. "But I think of something my grandpa told me: 'A long life is never good enough, but a good life is long enough.' That's true, isn't it?"

"Yeah," I say, surprised to feel tears in my eyes, too.

We drive to Jonny's house to drop him off. "Thanks for coming to the funeral," I tell him. "It meant a lot."

"It was an honor," Jonny says.

"Bye, Jonny." I wave to him out the window.

\* \* \*

I'm watching the news on Sunday morning, not really paying attention, but something catches my ear: "Local teenage boy hit by a car on Saturday night and pronounced dead his morning. He has been identified as Jonathan Harris..."

My cereal bowl drops to the floor.

Mom hears the crash and rushes into the room. "What in the world?" She sees the caption on the television screen and encloses me in her arms. I break down in tears.

He was my best friend. We went through everything together. We were inseparable. He went with my family on summer vacations. I knew his siblings like they were my own.

I feel angry at him. Furious. I want to scream. How could he leave me like this?

The rest of the day unfolds in a blur. I wake up the next morning, and all I can remember is crying and being half-carried up to bed.

When I walk into the kitchen, everyone is gone except for Mom, who is sitting at the table with her back to me, sipping tea. The clock reads 12:07.

"How long was I out?" I say.

She jumps at my sudden presence. "About fifteen hours," she says. "I bet you're starving. Want something to eat?"

She makes me a plate of eggs and toast. And that's how my life without Jonny begins.

\* \* \*

Ten years later, I decide to go visit Jonny's grave. I am now twenty-seven years old and I live six hours away. But it's the anniversary of Jonny's death, and I need to go back.

Before I visit the cemetery, I stop by Jonny's old house at 1423 Oak Street. The house looks the same but a new, young family lives there. I drive down my old street. My old house and the neighboring houses, 1211 to 1215 Elm Avenue, are now a hotel and parking lot.

After a couple hours of aimless driving, I finally summon the courage to drive to the cemetery. I sit on the concrete bench by Jonny's grave, put there by his family.

"Hey, Jonny," I say. "It's been a long time, huh buddy? I'm married to a very fine lady now. Her name is Lisa. She's really sweet and pretty. You would like her." Before I know it, I'm talking to Jonny like the old days, telling him everything that happened since I moved away. And how I still think of him all the time. How despite all the happiness I've found, I never feel truly at peace. How every time I hear about a car wreck, my heart still seizes up.

"Jonny," I say, tears streaming down my face. "I have to tell you something. It's time for me to move on. Live my life. I have to tell you this... I have to say..."

I'm sobbing so much that it's hard to choke out the words. Finally, I do:

"Jonny, I have to say... goodbye. I will miss you forever. Bye, Jonny."

*Josiah Rood is fourteen years old and wants to go to medical school to become a doctor. He has one younger brother, one older sister, and is a Southern Baptist. He also has played the violin since fourth grade.*

# Beauty Is...

*by Jesse Rubin*

The radiant sun shines through the curtain and lands directly on my barely opened eyes. Combined with the noise of my alarm clock, it slowly forces me to rise from my enticing bed and prepare myself for the outside world. I pull on my dreary school uniform and inspect myself in the mirror on my door. I try to find a word in my head that perfectly describes my appearance: cute, pretty, maybe even beautiful, but with a sigh, I realize that none of these words fit. I lower my head from the mirror as the right word flashes through my thoughts: plain.

I make my way downstairs to where my mom is eating. My mom and my dad divorced when I was very young, and my dad did not even try to claim partial custody of me. I have no brothers or sisters, so I guess he just thought of me as his plain mistake. My mom works as a teacher and I haven't seen my dad in seven years, so I have no idea what he is doing.

My dad is a mystery to me, and I have absolutely no plans to try to solve it.

"Good morning, darling," my mother says, smiling.

"Morning." The word comes out of my mouth like a slimy slug. I flash her a smile. My mother's beautiful smile shows no resemblance to my dull, plain one. "Do I look beautiful today?" I ask her, just as I do every morning, and this time I give a little half-hearted twirl.

My mom's smile changes from one of happiness to one that holds many secrets. She says, just as she does every morning, "True beauty is something that you can only find in yourself."

The toaster next to my mom goes off and two pastries pop out. "You should be going to the bus now," she says. I grab the warm pastries out of my mom's hands, and slowly make my way down the street to my bus stop. After a few minutes, the big yellow vehicle drives up and I quickly walk in and take my seat in the middle. Just like every day before it, I slowly sink into the depths of the crowd, being seen, but not truly being known. I watch as all the good-looking, popular girls and boys pass me by. I yearn to be like one of them. As always, they pass me by without a backward glance in my direction. This would make me sad, but I have experienced it many times before. The only thing I can do is push my feelings to the side, and try to push on through the day. I hate how all of the small things that I shouldn't even be hoping for make me extremely sad or angry. The rest of the day slowly fades by, as it does every day, and I am back home before my mind realizes that the day is, in fact, over.

Dinner is boring as usual, and conversation is extremely rare. There are so many subjects that are off limits, like my dad, and money. My entire life is regulated to such an extreme point that I feel like I don't even have a grasp on it. Dinner passes even more quickly than school, and before I know it I am lying down in my bed waiting for sleep to overtake me. I rest my head on my clean, white pillow, and allow myself to drift into peaceful slumber.

The room slowly fades around me until it is all a mix of amazing colors, each one a miracle in itself. They are all beautiful, but when they are mixed together, they create something that seems beautiful and whole, like it is satisfied. The room disappears all together, until I am standing in a patch of white, with another circle of white around it, and another after that. This most simple pattern goes on and on, stretching forever, which I can see, even with my clouded human vision.

The white bleeds into the materials of the universe, until it has formed a landscape filled with many awe-inspiring things. There is a huge beach, but the water is a muddy gray color. There is a large series of buildings resembling the White House, but with a huge crack running down the side. A large area of a once amazing-looking suburb is flattened and burned to the ground, with the sky gray and ash flying through the air. There are many things in this wonderful yet beautiful place, so many that my mind struggles to remember all of them. I know they are somewhere in my mind, because each image is permanently stained upon it, but I struggle to find each of them.

All of these things pass by in a flash, but for me it stretches for an eternity. I see the faults in each of them. There is the crack, the horrible water, the blasted surface, and many more. The faults pass just as the whole images do. They fade into the back of my mind, and everything that I saw in this wonderful dream is brought forward again, not individually, but as a collage with all of them side by side, constantly moving. The only thing that never changes is a small black image, still and beautiful all by itself.

I slowly walk forward, into and away from an endless horizon of white. I fall into the still place and the entire collage starts moving faster and faster. Each small image might not have been beautiful, but together they make something so beautiful that eyes cannot register it. It is the entire world, all fitting together harmoniously. Everything falls in upon itself, and the collage disappears.

I wake up with a jolt, sweat streaming down my face. I brush my teeth, shower, and put on my clothes. I stand in front of my full-length mirror and smile. I know the word that describes me today.

I walk downstairs and eat my breakfast. As I am walking out the door, my mom stops me. "Don't you have something you want to ask me?"

"Nope," I say with a smile and make a clicking noise with my teeth. "I already know the answer to my question." I open the door and leave the house with a smile, which is mirrored on the amazing face of my mother.

I sit down in my usual seat on the bus, and I glow with a deep radiance. Everyone on the bus seems to notice me, but as usual, they say nothing, just let me relax in my solitary state.

The good-looking, popular boys and girls walk by me, and instead of blending in with the wall, I seem to shine brighter than any of them. As usual, they don't look at me, but I know that I don't really want to talk to them. My word comes back to me then: beautiful. I am truly beautiful.

*Jesse Rubin is a thirteen-year-old boy who resides in California. He has wanted to be a writer since he was very young. He is an avid reader, and aspires to be an author because through literature he feels he can make a massive impact on others.*

# Anyone Can Make It

*by Emily Saunders*

As my daughter blows out the candles on her eighteenth birthday cake, I feel sad. Happy but sad. People grow up too fast, especially the ones you care for. Especially the ones you love.

I take a picture of Alice as she cuts the cake and smiles at me. It's amazing how such a beautiful, wonderful, talented person can emerge from such a tough life. She was five when her father left. It was hard. Fortunately we had family and friends who helped us when we struggled. And Alice made it. She is so strong and smart.

When Alice was born, her father and I started fighting. The fights left me feeling bitter. Even now, they are painful to remember. We fought over money. Alice's father, Jacob, wanted to control all our money. I wouldn't get so much as an allowance, and neither would Alice when she got old enough for such things. I told Jacob it wasn't fair – I was the one who worked, after all. But Jacob wanted to control us. He believed Alice and I were his "property," meant to do what he wanted. He was so different from the man I had married. It tore our family apart.

When Jacob and I divorced, we went to court for child custody. Every day, I am thankful that I won full custody. It was a hard time for us though. Jacob still hates me, and he and Alice aren't close at all.

Alice is going off to college in two months, to Washington State. She wants to become a veterinarian. I am so proud of her. Her life has been difficult. Her father used to beat her when he got drunk or she disobeyed him. He beat me, too. Even in kindergarten, Alice was smart for her age and I think she could tell what was going on. She became my strength. She was so strong, even then.

"Mom? Are you okay?" Alice asks, seeing tears in my eyes.

"Everything is just fine," I tell her. "It is amazing how much you have been through, yet you have pulled through it all with a smile on your face."

"Thanks, Mom," Alice says, blushing. She is so modest.

"Now go ahead and open your gifts, sweetheart." I wipe my eyes.

She smiles and picks up a present. As the wrapping paper falls away, she lets out a small gasp. It is a gold necklace with a small diamond heart pendant. It was a gift to my mother from my father. Mom passed it down to me when I got married. Now, I think Alice deserves it.

"Oh, it's beautiful! Thank you so much, Mom!" Alice puts on the necklace. It complements her blue eyes perfectly. I stand up and give her a hug.

"To my perfect daughter," I whisper, "who is a source of strength for me always." We sit there, hugging each other, neither of us wanting to let go.

*Emily Saunders is an eighth-grader at Sidney Middle School in Ohio.*

# Oblivious

## *by Chloé Sehati*

There's a quote from an ancient Hebrew tale that teaches, "A blessing is a curse, and curse is a blessing." In other words, you can find positive solutions in negative situations, and vice-versa. I never believed it for a second, until my dad almost lost his life to a brain aneurism.

"What is an aneurism?" you might ask. Well, I asked the same thing. What happens is a blood vessel can thin out in a small section, forming a bubble. If the bubble bursts, the blood floods the tissue around that area; this is an aneurism. Now, if this blood goes back into the blood stream, it can go into the heart or brain and cause a blood clot. This can happen anywhere inside the body. If it clots the heart, it's called a heart attack. If it clots the brain, it's called a stroke.

It happened on one of those gloomy Sunday mornings that seem to last all day. I was eight, a second-grader, and eating breakfast with my sister, Desireé. Our mom was in the shower; our brother, André, at a cousin's house; and our dad was exercising in the garage.

Desireé and I were sitting at the edge of the long wooden dining table in chairs too big for us with over-sized bowls of cereal placed between our arms, laughing every time the other one stuffed another spoonful in her mouth. Then, with food stored in our cheeks, one of us would try to get a few words out, constantly flinging bits of cereal this way and that. The garage door was open a slight crack, and my sister stopped giggling for a moment, tilting her head. "I think Dad needs me," she said. Sure enough, I heard a weak, "Desireé," coming from the garage.

I continued chewing and watched as she slipped out of her seat, strode into the garage barefoot, and after a moment fast-walked back over to me.

"Dad's on the floor," she told me. "He said to get Mom."

"Then go get her. What happened?"

"Chloé, I told you, Dad's lying on the floor. He said to get mom."

Puzzled and still eating, I stayed where I was while my sister went to retrieve our mom. When she came back, instead of sitting at the table again, Desireé went back to Dad in the garage.

"Dad... is it an emergency?" she asked.

He struggled, slowly answering, "Y-e-s." I couldn't see anything going on. I didn't even comprehend the situation. Next thing I knew, Mom was in her towel with suds all over her hair, kneeling next to Dad. I stood right next to her, observing the scene.

My dad is a tough guy. He goes by two names: Joseph and Sharam. He has a sensitive personality, but he's buff, a businessman, knows more than anyone would need to know about nutrition, and is my invincible superhero. But in that moment, I knew something was very wrong. I remember looking down at him and watching him answer my mother's questions.

"Are you okay? What's going on, Sharam?" My mom couldn't keep her voice from sounding scared. Never in my life had I seen her like this.

"My... head... hurts," Dad replied. He could barely speak. It was almost as if the dictionary in his mind were being torn out page by page. He was on his back, motionless.

"Where does it hurt? Can you show me?"

"Uh... no... there." His voice was muffled and every word faded once he got it out.

"Do you need to go to the hospital?" Mom was getting nervous.

"Yes." My dad doesn't go to the doctor unless he really needs to. To him, fruit is his medicine unless he needs prescription medication; there's always another solution besides treatments. When he said he needed to go to the hospital, I knew things were seriously bad.

My mom tried to get him up and into the car, but he could barely move. She asked if she should call 911, and he said, "No." I just had to stand back and watch all of this with my sister. When Mom tried lifting Dad, it was too much for her. She finally realized the only thing left to do was to pick up the phone and push three buttons.

The next part isn't completely clear and seems like a dream; I was in a daze the entire time. Here's what happened:

Eyes: I saw my frantic mother with the phone pressed hard to her ear, and her eyes, fearful, glued to my frail father; her mouth moving constantly; my sister's tears; my dad, just lying there, waiting for... for what? I saw my curious neighbors slowly coming out of their houses in socks and slippers while the fire department rolled in, followed by the paramedics, followed by the police. I saw my barking innocent-looking poodle being shooed inside the house by our neighbor, Jackie, who came to help. And the last thing I saw? A bunch of men in uniforms crowding my dad, heads bent, hands working to heal, and the garage door being slammed in front of my face.

Feeling: I didn't know what stress truly felt like until then. Everyone was tense. I sensed everything changing, everything going wrong. The things jogging through my mind that day seemed like light switches all connected to one light bulb. For example, if I could hear my surroundings, I was blind and had no wisdom of anything to do with my body at that moment. I felt mute on the outside with loose worries swarming inside my head. My stomach kept knotting up, and I felt sick. I was shivering all over.

Ears: I heard crying and questions being answered through the phone. I made out whimpers of uncertainty coming from my sister and me, from our neighbors, and from my mom. I perceived the sounds of muffled sheets carefully being wrapped around my dad like a crease-free gift, the soft footsteps of the paramedics, and a crisp silence from those just staring at everything that was happening.

Taste: My mouth was dry and I had a complete loss of appetite. I could taste acids from my stomach coming back up a little bit due to nervousness.

Smell: I still remember the scent of that scene, but I haven't been able to place the same one again because it was so extraordinarily different from anything I have ever experienced. The air gave off a waft all of the emotions around me as if they were bundled up in a bubble and popped in front of my face, and the aroma was a combination of fear and nerves and uncertainty.

The doctors and nurses at the local hospital decided to send my dad to the UCLA hospital by helicopter. Desireé and I were sent to my aunt's house with my brother and cousins. I was told that my father had a headache.

The next day, a Monday, I went to school. Somehow, the world went on despite everything. My mom still wasn't home. The babysitter, Lulu, was helping us out. All of the adults around me were concerned and asked about my dad, saying things like:

"Oh, how's Joseph?"

"Is Sharam doing okay?"

"Chloé, I'm so sorry about what's happening to your dad."

I had no idea Dad was in Los Angeles, and I really didn't understand the severity of the situation. At school, the teachers bothered me, asking if I was "okay" and if my dad was "okay." I was sick of it. He was fine! Then, two or three days later, one of the teachers asked me when my dad was getting surgery. That did it for me – there was something I didn't know.

Here's how my mom's schedule went: Wake up early, go to UCLA, and come home in time to tuck us in, just to wake up early again the next morning and go back to L.A.; on and on. The night after my teacher's question, I asked Mom what was happening to Dad. She finally decided it was time to sit down with my brother, sister and me and tell us. We all settled ourselves in the living room: children on the couch and mother half-leaning-half-sitting on the coffee table in front of us. She told us that Dad had an aneurism and explained it the best she could. She explained he was in the UCLA hospital and that the doctors needed to do surgery. The operation would take fifteen hours to complete and involved shaving his head completely; therefore "he will look a little scary afterwards." Also, the aneurism happened in a section of his brain that sent signals to the body for speech and movement, so he would be in a wheelchair and would need to practice talking and writing for a while. "But he will be okay," she said.

Whoa! I suddenly became a sponge, taking in everything at once and somehow keeping it all inside of me. I felt overwhelmed. I may have even gotten my first wrinkle.

The day *finally* came that we could see Daddy. The drive to L.A. that Friday afternoon right after school felt longer than a journey across the Pacific Ocean and back. I remember my mom steering our red Suburban into the large parking structure. She told the man in the window that we were visiting Joseph Sehati and he let us in. The walk to my dad's room felt lonely. My footsteps echoed with my brother's and sister's on the tile floor. There were white-coated doctors and nurses with pinned-up hair and clipboards. Finally, we stopped in front of a room on the left-hand side of the hall that read "Sehati" on the door.

Dad was sitting in a chair in the corner of the bland room with a beanie on, and his smile was so wide and happy. He looked pale, but his eyes were twinkling and tearing up; he could barely say hello to us because he was so choked up. When he spoke, he stuttered a bit but he tried so hard to make everything seem normal that we knew we had to just nod along; we pretended like nothing was much different, the best actors we could ever be. When the three of us walked up to him, he hugged us all in one great big bear hug, his arms wrapping tightly around us. I looked at him up close and realized how fragile he had become. When he pulled off his beanie to show us the scar left over as a souvenir from the surgery, I was shocked. There was a line of swollen stitches crossing the right side of his head, and all of his hair was shaved off. There was a little bit of fuzz growing, and the worry lines on one side of his forehead were gone; it was smooth, slick and shiny.

We left about fifteen minutes later when a nurse came in to check on him. She had a needle in her hand. It seemed completely routine to him but to me... well, I was not sure how to act. My siblings and I followed Mom out into the hallway, waving goodbye to Dad. The entire time, our faces had a plastic coat over them, and no one could see through us. We were no longer the translucent children we once were... we transformed into actors and actresses.

When Dad arrived home, he brought a wheelchair, walker, and cane with him. I think I even saw him shake a little bit, but he had decent strength; he was my healing Superman. When he was awake, he practiced his physical therapy stretches, writing techniques, and speaking strategies, but pretty much all he could do at first without getting too exhausted was eat and sleep; he only went out of the house for physical therapy classes and check-ups. We had a sign over the doorbell asking to "Please knock quietly," and the phones were always on an impossibly low volume on the opposite side of the house. Everything spoken was always in whispers. Suddenly we had random gifts and visitors all the time.

Now that my dad was home, all of us – my mom, brother, sister, Lulu and I – felt like his guardians. We spent time with him as much as we could and told him we loved him even when he was napping. We realized how much we took for granted before this experience, and we were thankful for all of the happiness that had been restored in our lives. Dad's quickly improving health became a miracle and all of the negative energy that filled us up before transformed into joy and relief.

My father having an aneurism taught me that positive things can come from the worst experiences. This all tracks back to the passage, "A blessing is a curse, and curse is a blessing." When my dad was fourteen, he walked through the front door of his house after school one day to discover that no one was home. He found out from a nanny assisting with household chores that his father was unconscious in the hospital after having a stroke, and the whole family was there with him. Two days later, he found himself standing next to his father's delicate body on a lonely hospital bed with no choice but to say goodbye. Just like that, he lost his father. My grandpa having a stroke was a curse, but it was also a blessing because it made my dad realize that he cannot take anything for granted and that, in fact, nobody should.

It is terrifying to think that I could have lost my father, too. I feel blessed that my dad is fine now. I know it sounds corny, but love does overpower every force imaginable. When the aneurism first hit him, my whole life seemed ruined; but the experience helped me become the person I am today. I realized that I need to do the best for myself and have strength, no matter what hits me. The best lesson my dad has shared with me is, "Every teeny, teeny, tiny second matters."

*Chloé Sehati was born and raised in Ventura, California with her triplet siblings André and Desireé. She is a freshman at Ventura High School and has had a passion for writing since the first grade. This is her first published work.*

# The Perfect Dance

*by Kayleigh Sephton*

The day is dawning,
The sun is rising,
You grasp every ounce of one tender dream.
Hold on to it tightly because it's fragile,
Now move intentionally into that room
Where dreams come true.
You only need one room, one studio,
To become you.

The blood, sweat and tears will fall in the midnight
hour,
With every tender step of practice needed,
Your spirit feels a heartbeat racing,
Don't let in decrescendo.
Because with every pounding heartbeat,
The passion in your spirit will soar;
So add the flames of burning passion
That everyone will see in your eyes.
See it in your own eyes now,
With every move reflected back at you.

Gently stir in the glistening diamonds of elegance,
So that every move now
Becomes accentuated perfectly.
The moment is here and now,
Your solemn tears fall gracefully,
As it becomes clear
The most important ingredient is you.

Let the midnight hour become your spotlight.
As your piano begins to play,
Let the melody take you away,
Your stage is set,
The practice is over.

Never lose yourself,
Find yourself in every move,
Through the music,
Create the perfect dance!
Feel the passion burning,
The spotlight shining,
The practice paying off,
And the dream coming true.
Dance!

*Kayleigh Sephton was born in England and moved to Arizona at age thirteen. It was a difficult move and making friends was hard, but over time she has settled in. Her love for writing, music and dance keeps her strong.*

# Jesusita Fire

### *by Hailey Sestak*

On Wednesday afternoon
in the mountains of Santa Barbara
the fire began.
No time for evacuation preparation.
Not a chance to make plans.

Difficult to pretend like everything is okay
when it feels like the Jesusita Fire
is here to stay.

The world seems to have come to an end.
The fire does not know when to stop.
We cannot defend
all the homes and lives.
You can hear the town cry.

Half the town is burning.
My friends' houses are gone.
Nothing left.

I can't stop thinking,
what if my house wasn't here?

Life isn't always fair.

My family and I gather
in the living room
to watch.
On the news, Channel 703,
we see eyes crying, hearts dying
for the loss of the beautiful Santa Barbara
we knew.

*Hailey Sestak moved with her family from Minnesota to California when she was eleven years old. Now, she is a sophomore in high school. She participates in four theater productions a year so she is almost always busy rehearsing or performing!*

# Those Eyes

*by Katelynn Smith*

I see your eyes and wonder
What they are saying.
For they are proud as thunder,
But it's a game they are playing.
For an instant they are at peace,
And the next they flare.
When will this game cease?
I don't think it's fair.
One moment I see pure desire,
Then suddenly it flees.
The skills I just can't acquire,
To read those eyes I see.

*Katelynn Smith is a young, aspiring writer with big
dreams who lives in a small town in Indiana. Hanging
out at the lake with a book in her hand and lemonade
at her side is one of her favorite things to do.*

# Smiles

*by Natalie Smith*

My smile is golden,
It fits me perfectly.
I live in smiles,
The way my lips change shapes.
I live with braces,
The way they've changed my face.
Tight lips, fake smiles, the
Occasional Cheshire-Cat Grin.
My smile is golden,
It fits me perfectly.
I smile at nothing and everything:
At friends,
At basketball,
At music,
At boys.
Most of all,
I smile at me.
My smile is golden,

It fits me perfectly.
I smile to live
And live to smile.
Do you live in smiles?
The way they give you butterflies?
Do you smile when you run?
Sing?
Sleep?
I do.
I laugh in smiles.
I love in smiles.
I live in smiles.
Because my smile is golden
And it's made just for me.

*Natalie Smith is fourteen years old and lives in Ventura, California. Her favorite activities include playing basketball, playing the cello and bass, hanging out with friends, and writing.*

# My Journey

*by Isabella Spaulding*

Can you imagine what it feels like to look forward to something with all your heart, only to have your high expectations left unfulfilled? As an immigrant in the late 19th Century, I know this feeling of sorrow. Traveling across the Atlantic Ocean in steerage, seeing the Statue of Liberty for the first time, and making it through Ellis Island's puzzling inspection process were bittersweet experiences for me.

I had to live and sleep in the steerage of the ship for six weeks, among the stench of sickness and horrible smell of many unwashed bodies. The rotten food reeked like a pile of dead fish that had been left in the sun for weeks. Looking around, I saw my temporary home as stuffed as everyone's suitcases. Everyone wore rags, their faces streaked with dirt. I had a terrible feeling that if I didn't get off that ship, I would become sick like the poor passenger next to me. If I got sick, I knew I might never make it to America.

When the vile voyage finally ended, everybody ran to one side of the deck. The fresh, slightly salty ocean air breezed past my face, and my excitement grew as I gazed out at freedom, the colossal green lady. I knew this had to be the Statue of Liberty, a symbol of America. It seemed that she held up her flaming torch to welcome me into her country as I struggled to hold back my tears of joy.

Slowly, we all departed the ship and walked onto an island where we were overshadowed by a giant stone building. Fear built up inside me as I walked through the doors and into a huge room bursting with people from every place on Earth. I noticed inspectors deciding whether or not the immigrants who stood before them would pass through to America or be forced to remain on the island for further tests. I heard the echoes of an abundance of languages as we were herded through the lines like livestock. I wondered what it meant when the person next to me was marked with chalk – the same person who had been coughing beside me during my journey.

The inspectors prodded, poked, and asked ridiculous questions like, "How do you wash stairs? Bottom to top or top to bottom?" Finally, after all of the tests and questions, I was given a landing card and permission to enter New York.

Although not all of my high hopes were reached, I have finally made it. The horrid steerage, the Statue of Liberty representing freedom, and the nerve-wracking inspections at Ellis Island were all a part of my bittersweet journey. I don't know whether I will ever see my homeland again, or what I am going to do now, but at least I am finally here in America.

*Isabella Spaulding is a sixth-grader at Irving Middle School in Lincoln, Nebraska. She enjoys reading, ballet and playing the viola.*

# Broken Glass

*by Mekalyn Steve*

It wasn't as much the cold, icy wind that numbed my body; rather, it was fear that twisted my nerves and froze my lips. I was abandoned, sundered from the only family I had ever known. I sat outside the run-down beach shack I still called my home. The sounds and flashing lights were still so visible in my mind as they toppled over one another like the giant balls of tumbleweed that rolled across the roads. There had been men outside wearing official blue suits with little objects and badges all over them. They carried something, though I never did know what it was, and it made my parents raise their arms in fright. The men bound my parents' hands in metal cuffs and shoved them into big flashing beasts whose feet rolled along the dirt and disturbed the murky water settled in the indents of the road.

"Hide in the closet," my mother had urgently said to me with a heavy voice. "Don't let them find you."

*Why? Why couldn't I be found? Was I an embarrassment?*

"No!" I yelled as they slammed the doors. I ran out the back door and through the underbrush that attempted to tangle up my scrawny legs. It wasn't long before I became powerless in the ocean of tall, dead grass and I tripped. My face hit the mud and I stayed there, feeling like a hopeless seed embedded in the ground. Of course, every seed needs to be watered and the skies complied, raining harder and harder. The rain drenched my long, uncombed hair and was almost loud enough to drown out the sirens and the shouts from my house up the hill. I was alone, undiscovered, and wet.

My tears fell involuntarily just as the sky bled red, orange, and purple. It was as if a can of colorful paints was overturned on a bluish canvas and dabbed with cotton balls that had been soaked in the sea. Numbness swept over my body and left me with severe fatigue. My eyes closed slowly and I hoped they would never open...

A sound awoke me and I opened my eyes to see a woman standing there, staring at me. I must've looked like a crunched up piece of paper that was thrown out of a car window onto the side of the road. Neither of us said a word and my lips were too frozen to even breathe a sigh of relief. I had been found.

\* \* \*

"Linda" was what she said her name was. I didn't know if I liked it, but I did know I liked being out of the cold. Just like my parents, I had been put in one of the beasts with feet that rolled, except this one was red and shiny and there were no flashing lights on the top. I had seen pictures of these beasts in magazines my mom had brought home. I was never allowed to go outside the bounds of our property and there were many things that the beast went past that were unfamiliar to me.

The beast, which Linda said was called a "car," stopped in front of a large, looming building with the words Meyer's Children Orphanage in bold letters at the top. Linda opened the car door and helped me out, escorting me up the steps. Once inside, I was taken to a tall desk in the center of the room where a slightly plump lady with glasses smiled with a tired expression.

"I found her alone about a hundred feet from the road. If you ask me, I think she was abandoned," Linda told the lady at the desk. Then she whispered to her, "Actually, there was a story on the news this morning about a man and woman busted for drugs. They lived in the shack near where I found her. I suspect they were her parents."

"What is her name and age?" the woman asked. Linda looked down at me as if expecting me to answer. I just stared at her with big eyes.

"I'm not sure what her name is, but I'd guess she's about seven years old." The woman at the desk scribbled down something on a piece of paper and smiled at me.

Within the next few minutes, I was taken upstairs, away from Linda, and given my very own bed on the third floor. It was only a little wooden frame with a thin mattress, but it was nicer than anything I had ever slept on, so I pounced on it eagerly. Then I was alone to study the room. There were ten other beds lined up side-by-side like the plants my dad had grown in the back of the house. The walls had a pinkish hue and there was a long crack in the ceiling. It was all so strange to take in. My body still felt numb.

A few hours later, I heard a bustle of footsteps coming up the stairs and a mob of young girls streamed through the door, talking excitedly to teach other. It only took them a few moments to realize that I now occupied the once-empty bed in the corner. Most of them just stared, and then one girl came forward. She looked to be a couple years younger than me.

"What's your name?" she asked.

"Ally," I whispered shyly.

"Hi, Ally! I'm Sasha Bently!" she said gleefully. She looked at the others. "And that's Sarah, Casey, Molly, Bridget, Peggy, Morgan, Ana, Lexi, and Jordan. It's great to meet you. Did you just come here? What happened to your family?"

Sasha looked so innocent standing there with her little pigtails bobbing up and down. The rest of the girls stood behind her, waiting for me to answer. I mustered up my courage and explained to them what happened to my parents and how I didn't know where they went. When I was finished, I felt as if a weight had been lifted off my frail shoulders.

The tall girl named Bridget said suddenly, "They took them to jail? That's awful!"

I didn't understand what she meant and I didn't feel like asking. Just then a bell rang twice and I was shoved through the door and down the stairs to the dining room where two very long tables were surrounded by chairs. Several platters of food were set on the tables as other boys and girls came rushing down the stairs to take a seat. The mouth-watering aromas enticed me towards a table. I sat down next to Sasha. The food tasted heavenly, and most of the time was spent shoving food into my mouth as if I hadn't eaten in years and avoiding the awkward stares of the other children.

When everyone was done, we were taken back upstairs to go to bed. It was difficult adjusting to the surroundings, but before long I had fallen fast asleep.

The next morning, I woke to the soft rush of air coming in through the window combined with an unfamiliar padding of feet against the wood floor. I sat up to rub my eyes and was intrigued to see a small, white cat with a round black nose, as if it had been dipped in paint. There were nearly invisible paw prints leading from the door to my bed. The white cat curled up comfortably on the thin mattress. I stroked its fine fur as it purred.

An hour later, the cat had gone and almost all the girls were up rushing around, throwing their jackets over their shoulders as defense from the harsh wind that shook the trees outside. I was the last one out the door. It was mainly because I couldn't properly fasten the fancy buttons on the new clothes I was given to wear at the orphanage. I'd never been taught how to button my old rags.

I wasn't hungry for the steaming blueberry pancakes that covered the table so I watched the others drizzle warm maple syrup over them and eagerly gorge themselves. I was fascinated by the intricate display of expensive china and glass objects around the room. It was all so fancy and unreal. And here I was, a ragged mess, amidst the finery.

Later that day, there was a game of soccer and even though I had never played the game in my life, I enjoyed kicking the weathered ball around.

The week passed, full of games and food. It was fun, but still I felt lonely and out of place, as if there was something missing or forgotten. It wasn't until three weeks later that I began to realize what these feelings were all about.

\* \* \*

The sun was just creeping up to peek though the window when I was shaken awake. I looked up to see Linda standing over me. "Good morning, Ally," she said. "How are you feeling?"

"Good, I guess," I said mumbling. I rubbed my sleepy eyes for a moment.

"Well, Ally. I've got some news for you: I'm taking you home with me." I was flooded with confusion, but I put on the clothes she had brought for me and followed her downstairs to the desk. There was a different lady there now and she said, "Congratulations on being adopted, Ally!" before we walked out the door and into the shiny red beast once again.

Linda smiled at me as we moved down the road, past the grove of dancing trees and the lush honeysuckle from which hummingbirds collected sweet nectar. Linda looked beautiful. She wore pearl earrings and her hair was up in a tight bun with an intricate flower pin clipped in the side. Her clothes, like the ones I wore, were marvelously fancy and there was an elegance about her that I had never seen before.

Thirty minutes later, the shiny red beast stopped in front of a large mansion with a white marble exterior and fountains outside. I almost had to convince myself that I had not died in my sleep and gone to heaven. Linda led me up the stairs, through the door, and up to a bedroom. Unlike my room at the orphanage, there was only one bed in the middle of the room with a pink satin bedspread and pillows that looked like fluffy, white clouds. There was a mahogany desk against the opposite wall and a dresser in the corner. And there was my very own window for only me to look through with silky curtains blowing and twirling in the breeze.

"Magical" was the only word in the whole world that could describe my new bedroom. It was truly magical. I opened the dresser to find a dozen dresses exactly my size. I pulled a black, velvety dress out of the drawer and put it on. I twirled all around the room with the ruffles flying. I felt like a princess.

"Welcome to your new home," Linda said softly. I smiled the biggest smile I ever have, and she smiled back. Then she left the room so I could settle down and relax. I walked over to the desk positioned against the wall and picked up a little circular mirror with a long handle. I stared into it and was shocked to see me – only it wasn't me at all. It was someone who looked like me in beautiful clothes and combed hair. It was a girl who had everything she could possibly want.

I set the mirror down. No, this wasn't me. I had nothing. *Where was I? Was the real me still sitting in the ocean of dead grass by the beach shack?* I couldn't stand not being me and not knowing where I had gone. It was as if I had ended my life and started another. It felt so wrong.

I slipped off the velvety black dress and took my old rags out of the bag I had brought with me from the orphanage. I put them on and sat down at my desk once again. I took the mirror and looked at my reflection. I had found part of me, but something still wasn't right.

I hit the mirror against the edge of the desk. I shook my hair around. Then, slowly, I lifted the mirror up once again.

There, I saw myself. The Ally I was so used to, covered in rags. But the mirror was shattered; my face was cracked into a dozen little pieces. This wasn't who I wanted to be, and it wasn't how I wanted to live.

*But how do you transition into a whole new life?*

I put the mirror down and looked out the window. A wave of green hills stretched in every direction.

Dark clouds protruded through the trees. I knew what needed to be done.

I slipped down the hall, past Linda who was preparing dinner with a man I assumed was her husband. I opened the front door to reveal my atrocious self to the world, heading to the garden to bury my face in the dirt.

Just like that sad day when my parents left, it began to rain. Before long, my hair and clothes were soaked. Except now, instead of becoming a useless, dying seed, I began to grow. I was fed by the earth and watered by the sky, and now I had the love I needed. I had Linda to take care of me.

I lifted my face from the mud just as a flower protrudes from the earth. Now I could mend the broken glass in my life to form a new image that was even more beautiful than before. It was the image of a new beginning; a new life; a new Ally.

*Mekalyn Steve is fifteen years old and was born and raised in Ventura, California. She has been writing stories, poems, and essays for as long as she can remember and has co-written a novel that she hopes to get published someday. She likes to include a meaning or lesson in all of her stories. When she grows up she hopes to continue producing meaningful works as a travel writer and photographer.*

# I Let Go Of You

*by Leighton Suen*

You see right through me, and not in a good way.
You don't know I exist; it's a typical day.
But to keep me hoping and dreaming for you,
You sometimes talk to me like you always knew
Who I was. You make me so confused.

So let go of whatever you think the problem is,
And pretend that you don't know what's wrong with
me,
Cause I know: deep inside of you, you must like me
too.

I hear you talking, talking about me,
But I just keep on walking, hoping you don't see,
And sometimes when you call my name
My heart stops beating, my cheeks go aflame.
I start hoping you meant somebody else
Then you look at me; I smile –
I bet you're pleased with yourself.

Was it all just my delusion?
Wasn't real – an illusion…
Tell me the truth; don't be scared I'll break
You'd be surprised at how much my heart can take.

\* \* \*

After a long long time, I started thinking of you
And what you did to me; it felt like centuries ago.
I wanted to call you – know what I would've said?
"It's been so long; Now I don't care a shred
After all those nights and imaginary tears that I shed,
My heart's no longer yours – my love for you is dead."

So I let go of what I thought the problem was
Now I know that there's nothing wrong with me
And I hope somewhere deep down inside of you,
That your feelings for me are gone, too.

*Leighton Suen is a fifteen-year-old high school student living in New York City. He enjoys writing poems to express his feelings and is inspired by almost everything he sees.*

# The Third World

*by Jack Swift*

It was a dark night. Everything was silent and still. I crept out of bed, sneaking past our sleeping cat, Rex. I tiptoed out the door, down the street, and gasped. In place of the nice railroad station was a dome. It appeared to be made of plastic. What looked like train tracks, but smaller, ran through the dome. The eerie building shone in the light of the moon.

Then I saw a shadow. I spun around. A small man stood before me. I took him to be an elf. I asked him what this place was. He gave a grunt and, after a while, said, "Well, this is the Railroad of the Worlds."

"The worlds?" I said.

"Of course," the mysterious creature said. "There are four worlds, but the fourth has been lost forever. Well, aren't you going to get aboard?"

I thought for a moment, then I followed the little man into the dome. I saw a vehicle hooked up to the tracks. It had a sail and looked very elegant. I stepped in and the elfin creature followed. The vehicle pulled away from the dome and shot onto the tracks like a bullet coming from a gun.

Soon we disappeared into the cold mist. When we came out we were in a rocky gorge. Scorpion-like creatures occupied the place and one came a little too close to the tracks. It was turned into road kill. I looked at the spinning wheels of the Railroad of the Worlds. Purple blood oozed down the wheels. Suddenly, one of the creatures leaped up and stung the elf. He fell into the gorge.

I was on my own. Fear crept up my body. I did not want to end up like the fallen elf. Once again I sailed through the mist. I came out in a dazzling shower of sparks. I was in the middle of a plush, green field whizzing along, not aware of what was awaiting me.

Just then, a huge worm-like creature shot up through the soft turf. I narrowly avoided being its evening meal. I now was aware of the danger and kept my head low. Once again we vanished into the mist. *This must be the Third World*, I thought.

When we came out of the fog I was falling. Then, everything went black and that's all I remember.

*Jack Swift grew up in a peaceful town in Southern California called Thousand Oaks. He lives with his parents, sister, and cats. He enjoys reading, writing, playing video games, and soccer.*

# Black And White

### *by Julie Angela Teichert*

"Reggie Cox here backstage at the Times Union Center."

The camera zoomed in to do a close up on the man talking. "A huge hit just this year with their new album, City Eyes just finished their performance onstage here tonight and, as I'm hearing, will be heading on to New York City tomorrow. I'm here now with City Eyes' lead singer Sam Reyes."

The interviewer paused half a moment to glance at the boy standing next to him; the camera shifted to show them both.

"Sam, you guys put on a great concert tonight."

The boy smiled. "Thank you."

"I was lucky enough to be in the crowd. It was amazing. You know, you guys have so much energy when you perform." He smiled and said, half-jokingly, "You must be exhausted right now."

"Yes."

"Sam, a year ago hardly anyone knew you guys existed. Did you expect your very first album to be such a huge hit?"

The boy didn't have to wait to think of an answer. For some reason, all interviewers asked almost identical questions.

"It was a complete surprise," he said, a bit of the Minnesotan accent he hadn't yet lost coming out in his words. "None of us expected it to be anywhere near as big as it has been. Eight months ago we were completely unknown; now we can't go out in public without someone asking for an autograph or picture or something."

"I'll bet you enjoy that."

The boy nodded, his face only betraying a s*light* bit of his disinterest. "Yeah, it's cool."

The interviewer went on. "This seems to be the turning point in your career. It's either forward or backward from here." He added something funny.

Sam Reyes smiled; it was a fake smile.

\* \* \*

The other band members, C.J., Dylan, and Mike, were busy in the midst of some computer game or other on their laptops. Sam had had enough of games already. Instead, he sat at the tour bus window, watching the scenery go by without truly seeing it.

*Do I really want this?*

Right now, back home, everyone was probably starting school or getting ready for it. Why did he miss the classmates he'd hardly ever talked to? He thought about what that interviewer Reggie What's-

His-Name had said yesterday. *This seems to be the turning point in your career. It's either forward or backward from here.*

Fame – and fortune – ahead; a normal life behind. Which was he going to choose? He'd thought he could have both, but now he was realizing that wasn't exactly the case. Which one? As he stared out the window, he remembered the last time he'd seen her.

* * *

She'd said goodbye to him after school on his last day home. He could see the excitement and something else – worry? – in her face.

"Don't forget about all of us, Sam," she'd said quietly, fearfully. "Please." She glanced up at him almost nervously. "We'll miss you."

Sam smiled. She was adorable, really. He would miss her – those light brown eyes, her happy face, her patient listening, her constant attempts to lift everyone up when they were down. She'd always supported him and the other guys.

"Courtney, don't worry. I'm not going to forget you." He laughed. "I'm not going to change *that* much."

She'd smiled back at him, but the worry had remained in her eyes. They'd both been silent a moment.

"I'm excited for you," Courtney had finally said. "It's happening – all the things you always wanted."

"Yeah," Sam had answered. "It'll be amazing."

* * *

"Sam, you're so lucky! You're famous and you're gonna tour the country! Man, I wish I was you!"

"Thanks," Sam had said for the ninth time. Everyone was telling him that. All through the rest of that day he'd continued to hear things like it from the kids at school. Most of them he'd hardly ever talked to before; some, he didn't even know their names.

It had been great though. Everybody had talked to him.

* * *

"We're almost there," one of the boys said. Sam would've noticed already – if he'd been paying attention – by the crowd of people lined up outside the front entrance of the building. Here for the concert *very* early.

It had been six months now since their album had been released...

* * *

"I hope you'll be happy," Courtney had said at lunch a couple days after the album had skyrocketed, and City Eyes had suddenly become one of the biggest bands in the country. "I hope..." She trailed off.

"Of course I'll be happy," Sam had answered, giving her a smile. "I am happy. It's all me and the rest of the guys ever wanted." He looked at her, his face becoming serious. "Courtney, you don't have to worry about me. I'll be fine." He smiled. She was so kind and perfect. It was sweet to be so worried about him.

\* \* \*

*What if?*

What if he left it all behind; just went home? He could imagine what it would be like now. For a time, everyone would want to talk to him. Everyone would want to know about the tour. Everyone would want to know why he left. For a while, he'd be the most popular person there. But then everyone's excitement would all wear out, and he'd be unnoticed all over again.

Courtney would still be there, though.

\* \* \*

She'd hesitated. She always hesitated before voicing her own opinion. "I just hope you don't get lost in everything. In all the people, the fame, yourself." She'd looked down worriedly. "I don't think you'll be happy that way, in the end."

"Don't worry. That won't happen," he'd promised.

\* \* \*

Someone in the crowd outside the concert hall realized who was driving by in the tour bus; all the people started screaming and waving. The boys waved and smiled back from the window, laughing to each other, or themselves, about it.

Before the days of City Eyes, unseen was all Sam had been. Not someone horribly unpopular, and not someone horribly popular. He'd been right in between, the kind of person not particularly cared about, thought about, or even noticed.

Sam smiled now, waved, and noticed that for any girl who realized he saw her, her day – no, her week – was instantly made. She started screaming louder and jumping up and down, probably hoping he'd notice her all the more, but by then she was out of his sight.

\* \* \*

Finally beyond the crowd, the bus was driving into the back parking lot, and it wasn't long before the boys were walking through the doors to the backstage area. Once in, there was suddenly another crowd, the usual crowd, surrounding them.

"We're working on a sound check now. You guys want to get onstage to see how it'll all work for the performance?"

"For the concert, you'll be onstage before the curtain goes up. As it's coming up, you'll begin playing."

"Security will walk out with you as usual."

\* \* \*

Before he'd been famous, who else had been there aside from his best friends, the other members of City Eyes? *There'd been Courtney, of course. She'd always been there.*

Sam glanced up at all the people moving around backstage. Whether doing sound check, working on security, ordering pizza for the boys, or walking around with a video camera recording all the hub-bub, everyone here was working for them, working on improving the setting of the concert.

Courtney was only one person. The way things were now, thousands of people knew him, noticed him. Courtney had known him before, but what did she know about this world here backstage? What did she know about this life?

Sam imagined it again. If he left this all behind, went back home, everyone would be so puzzled over why he'd left; rumors would fly. Why would Sam leave something he'd been working toward for so long? Was the fame all too much for him?

He knew everyone would stare at him for being the person who "had it all" and then left it behind. He winced. There was no way he was going back home to have *that* as his welcome.

And what about after those stares wore away? Everything would be normal again. He'd be unseen. Who would notice what he did? Who would care? No one. That was what it had always been like for him. Could he be happy like that again?

*No.* He gave it a half-second more thought, and reluctantly changed his answer to a *yes*. He could be happy. He'd go ask Courtney out. She'd been his friend for so long. Of course, with Courtney, he could be happy that way – unnoticed by everyone else. When they all looked right past or straight through him, Courtney would see the person there. She'd see him.

*Maybe that's what I should do. Go back home, go to Courtney, live a normal life. In the end, I'd be so glad I did it.*

He sighed. But what would everyone else think? So many would think he was weak. They'd call him weak for leaving, say he wasn't strong enough to bear the sacrifices, the pains you had to go through in this world of music and touring and screaming fans. That was stupid. He could show them easily enough. He could do more than just bear it; he could embrace it.

* * *

It was a half hour till the concert started. The band members were all together in one backstage room, each of them passing the time in whichever way he chose, all of them talking about how nervous they were. Sam sat in one of the sofa chairs, staring at the cream colored carpet at his feet, again not really seeing it.

What did Courtney know? What made her think this wouldn't make him happy? He glanced up. The guys were all joking around; these were his friends. They were smiling, laughing. How did Courtney know whether this would make him happy or not?

* * *

He'd missed hearing the "You're on in two minutes." They were on *now*.

Sam stood and led the way out the door and began the walk up the stairs to the front of the stage. Why should he go back to the way things were before? No, people were going to *notice* what Sam Reyes did. He had the chance to be recognized; he was going to be recognized. This career, this world here, this was what was important. Why did his life before matter? It was behind him. He wasn't going to let it hold him back; he'd leave it in the dust and get ahead.

He was about to step out onto the stage. *What about Courtney?* He stopped. Could he really leave her behind like she wasn't important? These screams, this stage – she'd always said that, alone, they couldn't make someone happy. He *knew* they weren't going to make him happy. There was so much more to life than this. So many more important things. He wasn't going to be happy with this, just this.

Still, here onstage, he'd be known.

Sam bit his lip and shrugged. Who was Courtney to say this wouldn't make him happy? What did she know about it? He didn't care; this was his choice. *I'm not going to go through life invisible, unrecognized. I'm not.*

He walked forward onto the stage, over to his microphone at the center. Courtney didn't think he'd be happy; he'd show her.

*Nothing else matters.*

He looked back to the others with a nod, and C.J. began the first notes of the song. Sam began singing as the curtain slowly went up.

The lights were bright, blinding him as he looked out over the crowd of people screaming and singing along.

This was it. This was the life he chose. *I'll probably hate myself for this choice later, but I'm not going back.* He looked out over the crowd again, the thousands of people, all their eyes on him. He was recognized. This was it.

\* \* \*

The door slammed shut; C.J., Dylan, and Mike were left in silence.

"What's *wrong* with him?" Mike asked. It was three years since their first concert in New York City. They were back there now, waiting for yet another performance to begin. Sam had just left the room.

"I don't know," Dylan answered, shaking his head. "Sam sees everything so black and white. It's only extremes for him."

C.J. shrugged. "I wish he'd realize he didn't have to leave everything important behind for this."

Dylan finally said what they were all thinking. "I wish he would go find Courtney again."

C.J. sighed. "I never saw anyone more miserable."

*Julie Angela Teichert is fifteen years old and currently in the ninth grade in California. She is the youngest in a family of eight. This is the first story she has had published; she hopes there will be many more to come.*

# Without You

## *by Cadie Underwood*

Dear Dad,
I want to tell you what a great life I've had
And thank you for all that you've taught me
And tell you what's happened to me recently.

You taught me what courage means
And not to hurt anyone's feelings;
A truck I have learned to drive
With you right by my side.

Without you I would not know how
To herd a sow or milk a cow;
I would not know that laziness is bad
I cannot imagine the life I would've had.

There is one thing I must tell you
If you are like me, you will cry too –
But please don't get depressed
Because the doctors have done their best.

The hard part to tell you is this
Before I seal my letter with a kiss:
Cancer is all over me
I am running out of time quickly.

This letter I had to write
Because I am full of fright;
I was afraid you did not know
That I love you so.

You have always been there for me
But sadly I have to go, you see –
Sincerely
Your daughter, Mary

*Cadie Underwood is a sixteen-year-old girl who was born and raised in Kentucky. She enjoys writing stories and poems along with caring for her animals on the farm.*

# The Accidental Valentine

*by Regina Vestuti*

*Dedicated to Diana Reeves*

In the gloom of night,
a ray of moonlight shone through prison bars.

A shadowed figure sat in sorrow
dreading the fate called tomorrow
missing his pale love.

The stale air brushed the cloaked figure
as she swept through prison containment
to her accidental valentine.

Through the night they waltzed to music unheard,
love hand in hand.

The birth of dawn as the bells chimed four
was the signal for the lovers to part.

The woman sat upon granite, weeping
tales of her love's horrid fate.

*Regina Vestuti is a ten-year-old living in Rhode Island.
She loves to read and make art projects. She has four
cats and all sorts of animals. She loves the ocean and
the mountains.*

# Mom

### *by Madison Watkins*

Mom is a person
Who cooks and cleans
And doesn't take no for an answer.

Mom is a person
Who blocks violence from the TV
And hugs you when you're hurt.

Mom is a person
Who loves you
Just the way you are.

Mom is a person
Who talks to you
When you feel down and blue.

Mom is a person
Who forgives your attitude
And forgets your mistakes.

Because Mom is a person
Who loves you
Truly and forever.

I love you, Mom.

*Madison Watkins is a twelve-year-old sixth-grader at Derry Area Middle School in Pennsylvania. She loves to write and draw and also enjoys basketball and soccer. One day she hopes to be a famous author!*

# The Blue Room

*by Gillian Wenzel*

Is there a poem in my room?
Where my clothes are strewn like noodles
And sand clings to the hardwood floors like
Memories, tattooed to its stable ground
Where standards of life are kept.
The concert hall where broken bands
Play from shiny speakers,
Coming alive once more.
The morning paper already devoured,
The books and pens, they lay out of ink;
Too many words to be written.
The artist's sanctuary with
Trinkets that contain stories.
This place that I sleep,
Then this –
This home that I wake to,
The blue room at the end of the hall
Has poems manifesting behind its doors.

*Gillian Wenzel is a fifteen-year-old freshman whose life is guided by her dreams. At age eleven, she sought to be published and her short story "We're In This Together" appeared in <u>Anthology of Short Stories by Young Americans (2006 Edition)</u>. She has a passion for writing, all things Italian, Stanford and the environment, but for the moment she is just trying to enjoy being fifteen.*

# Pygmalion's Galatée

*by Gillian Wenzel*

Hater, turned to lover
Because hard work pays
Hater, turned to lover
With manipulated clay
Hater, crying deeply
Let the stone love me back
Lovely maiden, perfect wife
No breath, no life.
Praying to the loving goddess
Let my love come alive
Flicker of fire
Flicker of hope.
He walks home to a possible bride
Find one lover stagnate; other one cries
He caresses cold marble with undying hope
Stone turns warm under gentle grope
Bride born from groom's hand
Born a love that will withstand.

*Gillian Wenzel is a fifteen-year-old freshman whose life is guided by her dreams. At age eleven, she sought to be published and her short story "We're In This Together" appeared in <u>Anthology of Short Stories by Young Americans (2006 Edition)</u>. She has a passion for writing, all things Italian, Stanford and the environment, but for the moment she is just trying to enjoy being fifteen.*

# Rain

### by Grace Euphrat Weston

Wet shivers wracked Iandra's whole body. The rain poured down, streaming together with her tears. Her cheeks felt wet and warm, then overly stretchy; the symptoms of a long cry. The news had arrived only half an hour ago.

"Honey." It was a statement, not a question. Iandra couldn't run away, but oh, how she'd like to. She set her backpack down, slowly. Perhaps if she tried to slow time down enough, it'd stop. Her mother spoke again.

"Iandra. I'm so sorry."

She never actually delivered the news, but Iandra could tell. She gasped. "D-Daddy?"

Mrs. Foraline's hands twitched, and she wiped down the counter as Iandra watched, her eyes following her every move. Finally her mother broke, and looked up from the brown stain she was viciously scrubbing. Her eyes had pooled with shiny tears. "Yes."

And Iandra fled, past the house, past the hospital, oh, past the hospital, down three streets, fleeing the glances the people gave her as they talked and laughed—and lived. Iandra fled from the living most of all; she was no longer a part of life, rather her spirit had run into her father's welcoming arms.

Yet her body sobbed on in the gutter, where the street and the sidewalk met, as the rain softly pooled around her.

*Grace Euphrat Weston lives in San Francisco and attends The Nueva School. In addition to writing, she enjoys reading and playing soccer.*

# Water-Bio Poem

*by Daniel Williams*

Water
Clean, fresh, delicious
Son of Minute Maid
Lover of Earth, environment, human bodies
Happiness in rivers, oceans
Fears sewers, fountains
Dirty, clean, disposed
Stocked in bottles, glasses, containers
Gives strength, fresh in taste
All over the world
Purified

*Daniel Williams is a published writer who lives in Indiana. He started writing when he was twelve years old.*

# Rosie's Grandma

### by Miguel Wise

"Grandma!" Rosie cried as she entered the room. Grandma was sitting on a rocking chair, staring into space.

"What?" Grandma said. "Who's there?"

"It's me," Rosie said, grinning as if it were a game. But Grandma did not go along with the game by saying, "Come here, my little Rosie." Instead she stood up and walked towards the door.

"Grandma?"

The door closed.

\* \* \*

"What happened to Grandma?" a confused Rosie asked her mother.

"I think we should leave her be right now," her mother replied. Rosie felt upset that her question had not been answered.

"What happened?" she asked again. Her mother wouldn't speak. They went into the car and drove home.

Rosie spent the whole night wondering what happened to Grandma. The next morning she asked her dad about her.

"Rosie," he said. "Grandma has Alzheimer's disease."

"What?" Rosie was confused. "A disease? You mean like a fever?"

"No Rosie, this is more serious. It's in her brain."

"You mean the brain can get diseases, too?" she asked.

"The brain can get many diseases," her dad said.

"What happens to someone with Alzheimer's disease?" Rosie asked.

Her dad answered uneasily, "A person has increased memory loss and problems with thinking, learning and speech until they can't care for themselves."

"Will Grandma get better?" Rosie asked. Tears began to run down her face.

"I hope so, but she might not," he said.

Rosie cried harder. Her dad hugged her tightly.

"How come all those problems happen when the brain gets a disease?" Rosie asked.

"The brain is the control center of the body," her dad explained. "The brain is told by special messengers called neurons about what is happening in the body and it sends messages to the body about how it should react. But the brain is also in charge of your thoughts, emotions, speech and the ability to learn, so when your brain cells get damaged all of those things get damaged."

"All of that can come out of something that looks like a wrinkly sponge inside my head?" Rosie asked.

"Yes, your brain is amazing," her dad replied.

* * *

Rosie continued going to her grandma's house. Grandma continually got worse. Eventually, Rosie's mom stopped taking her to see Grandma. Rosie worried about her, but her dad always reassured her.

After five months, Rosie received the sad news. Alzheimer's disease had finally taken Grandma.

Rosie wept. Her dad comforted her. "It was time for her to go," he said. "We should be happy for the good times we had with her."

Rosie felt better. She remembered all of the time that they had spent together and how happy they had been.

*Miguel Wise is an eighth-grader at University Charter Middle School in Camarillo, California. In his spare time he reads and writes; his passions are history and geography.*

# The Stuffing In The Bathtub

*by Naomi Wolfrey*

"I'm serious!"

"You can't be – that's impossible. You're crazy!" Erin stormed out of my room. She never believes a word I say. See, something crazy happened yesterday and you've got to believe me cause no one else will. I've had this teddy bear for as long as I can remember. And, don't laugh, but I sleep with it.

The other day, my aunt came back from a business trip in Paris. Usually Aunt Amber brings back really cool presents. Such as once she got me Guitar Hero III for my birthday, and another time she got me an awesome laptop from Italy. But I guess this time she decided to change her pattern. She got me a doll. And I don't mean a cheap plastic Barbie. No, I'm talking fancy porcelain with real hair and silk clothes. Yeah, it was expensive. So Aunt Amber really tried, but didn't get it right. Because I'm thirteen and I don't play with dolls. So it didn't have much of an effect on me. Of course, I thanked her, but I wasn't ecstatic about it. Then I brought Clarice, which is the doll's name apparently, to my room and set her on my dresser. Aunt Amber brought back some things for it – excuse me, for *her* – like a bed and pajamas, but I decided not to bother with that junk. I slipped on my pajamas, slid into bed, and went to sleep. But – and here's where the whole creepy part began – when I woke up, the doll, Clarice, was lying on the bed next to me.

I screamed.

Nothing. Either no one heard me or they were ignoring me as usual.

Then I realized my bear was gone. I shouted, "OMG where's Mr. Teddy Stuffing Stuffers? My number one BFF is missing!"

I tore up my room looking for him. (Not literally, of course – my mother would have a fit.)

I couldn't find him anywhere! I was seriously about to cry! Then I realized I hadn't checked the bathroom. *I bet Erin put him in there as a joke*, I thought. I rushed in, but then I stopped cold. Because there, in the bathtub, was Mr. Teddy Stuffing Stuffers. Surrounded by stuffing. With no head. I screamed again.

As I walked out of the bathroom carrying the headless body, and the head too, I said out loud, "If this is a joke, it's a really sick one." When I set him on the bed, I asked, "OMG Mr. Teddy, what happened?"

*Oh, yeah right,* I thought, *like he's going to answer me. He has no head!*

When I glanced over to Clarice, I noticed her delicate little hands had some white stuffing on them. And, for the first time that morning, I noticed some scissors on my nightstand. I screamed again, for the third time.

*Finally*, Erin came running in. I guess she was getting fed up with my screaming. "Steph, what happened?" she shrieked.

I said, "Look at Mr. Ted- I mean, my bear."

"Yeah, so what?" she said, shrugging.

"So what? So what! He's decapitated, that's what!"

"So? Throw it out," Erin said, disinterested.

"WHAT?" I exclaimed. "Never! He's my best fri – I mean, my earliest memory!"

"You're making way too big a deal out of this."

"No I'm not!" I insisted. "And I think Clarice did it!"

"Who?" Erin asked.

"The doll!" I said.

Erin gave me her doubting look. And that's where this whole story began.

So, Erin leaves, and I am alone again. Well, not completely alone. *She* – Clarice – is there, too. I run out of my room, screaming and clutching the wounded Mr. Teddy.

"Mom!" I shout. I run into her in the hallway. "Help me, please! Mr. Teddy's dying, do something!!"

She looks shocked and says, "Call nine-one-one! Where is he?"

"Um, right here!" I show her Mr. Teddy. I may have forgotten to mention that our next door neighbor's last name is Teddy, too.

Mom gets this somewhat annoyed look on her face and says, "Stephanie, it's a toy."

I frown. "Just help me, please!"

"Fine," she sighs. "I'll get my sewing kit."

"Yippee!" I give her a hug, then skip to my room. Guess where Clarice is? I have no idea, either! I flip out. I start looking around my room. When I open my dresser drawers, I shout, "Holy cabbage! Where are all my socks?"

I turn around and there is Clarice, napping on a pile of socks. I scream. (My voice is going to be very worn out soon.)

I gently lift her up and her eyes flash open. I guess she's one of those dolls that open and close their eyes. I set her little body down on the doll bed, and back up slowly. Her eyes close. Then flash open. Then close. Um, must be a glitch.

I set Mr. Teddy down on my bed, and then Erin walks in.

"Gee, Steph, Your doll looks kind of evil with that creepy smile on her face." Then she walks out.

I turn to look, and she's right. Clarice's once-innocent half-smile has been replaced by an evil grin. That's where I draw the line. I pick up the doll, chuck her into a nearby cardboard box and tape the lid closed. *Now that that's done with, I can go to bed.* So I do.

The next morning, I zip over to the box and open it. No doll.

I yell, "Mom! Did you take a doll out of this box?"

No answer. I stick my head down the hallway and yell again, "Mom?"

I hear laughter behind me. Creepy laughter. I turn, saying, "Huh?"

A scream, then silence.

*Naomi Wolfrey is twelve years old. She is an avid reader and enjoys writing. She also likes to act and play softball. Naomi lives in California with her parents, three brothers, and two dogs.*

# The Never-Ending Twinkle

*by Ruth Zurcher*

Roxanne didn't know that auditions were yesterday and now she had missed her chance. Ever since going to the circus when she was eight, she had been fascinated with the eating-fire technique. Roxanne frowned as she rested her head on her hands, sitting beneath her willow tree. Taz, her golden retriever, raced in circles around her.

"Taz," she said wistfully. "Do you think I'm a good fire-breather?"

The dog turned his head at the sound of his name and ran over to Roxanne, putting his head in her lap.

"I think you're a great fire-breather," said a voice behind her. Roxanne whipped her head around and saw a boy with a head full of chestnut curls and a grin on his face. His large, blue eyes seemed to have a never-ending twinkle in them.

Taz growled and rose to stand in front of Roxanne. The boy raised his hands, "I mean no harm." He put one of his hands in a pocket and pulled out a tube-like thing. He tossed it to Roxanne, waved with the other hand, and left.

Roxanne tucked the tube-like thing into her pocket. She had no idea what it was. She would inspect it later.

She thought about the boy during dinner. Her parents smiled at her and watched her get up after eating. They both had weird smiles on their faces and a twinkle arose in their dark eyes. "Good night, sweetie," they both said, synchronized.

Roxanne gave them a weak smile and left to her sanctuary: her room. Sitting on her bed, she pulled out the tube-like thing and inspected it. It was light blue and had a ribbon of gold around the top. At the bottom, it fanned out, like a bell, except crinkled. She put it to her lips and blew.

A burst of flame came out the fanned bottom and a circle of fire leapt in front of her. It was like a portal, and within it there was a moving picture. Roxanne saw herself, a bit older than she was and surrounded by gold coins and riches. She was blowing fire with something in her hand. Roxanne gasped and reached out in front of her. Mesmerized by the vision of her dream, she leaned forward and was sucked into the ring of fire.

A moment later, Roxanne found herself in a chamber, its walls holding back something behind chained doors. There were torches aligned on the wall and it was truly a ghastly place.

Roxanne felt a rush of fear and wrapped her arms around herself. Whatever was behind those chained doors, she knew, was projecting this fear. For whatever reason, she wanted to seek it out.

She walked towards the door, reaching out with her right hand, reaching for the doors. When her hand touched the doors, a rumble shook the chamber. She pressed her cheek against the cool wood and blew. A fire came out and began burning the wood. The chains melted and soon as there was an opening in the burned wood. Roxanne climbed through the hole and found herself face to face with a dragon. Shivering with fear and a strange excitement, Roxanne crept forward and watched the dormant dragon. She walked up to it and pressed her hand on its scaled forehead. It was cool, yet she could feel heat pulsing through its veins.

Its power surged through her and she began to transform. Roxanne grew taller and taller until the tip of her head was touching the high ceiling. Scales grew all over her body; her fingernails grew sharp and began to lengthen.

She landed with a *boom!* on the stone floor. She was a dragon. She knew it was meant to be all along. With the need to blow fire and the desire to fly – which had always been her wish every time she saw birds and kites – Roxanne had always known that if she had to choose to become an animal, she would choose a dragon.

The other dragon dissolved and right away Roxanne sensed fear again. Even though she was a dragon now, something didn't seem right.

Facing the burnt doors, a figure walked towards her, blowing out the torches that were her only light.

As soon as Roxanne saw the door reforming, she realized her mistake. The other dragon had been there, imprisoned for most of its life, protecting the treasures of one man.

She had been tricked. Rage swept through her and she tried desperately to catch something on fire. But now that the wood had already been burnt, it wouldn't burn again until the next wishful person came.

The figure reached the door and watched silently, with a grin on his darkened face, as the one free spirit was now tricked and trapped into protecting someone else's treasure.

The only light Roxanne could see was the never-ending twinkle of the boy's eyes that she could now only imagine.

*Ruth Zurcher is thirteen years old and goes to CAPE Charter School in Camarillo, California. She loves to write and encourage others to follow their dreams.*

# About Write On! For Literacy

Write On! For Literacy was founded by Dallas Woodburn in 2001 to encourage young people to discover confidence, joy, self-expression and connection to others through reading and writing.

Projects include:

- Annual Holiday Book Drive: as of December 2009, more than 11,200 new books have been collected, sorted and distributed to disadvantaged youth. Donation sites include Boys and Girls Clubs, Project Understanding, Casa Pacifica, and the Ventura County Migrant Education Services. We have been told that for many recipients, these books are the only gifts they receive.

- Writing Contests: categories of short story, essay, and poetry for young writers in elementary school, middle school, and high school. Gift certificates to bookstores are awarded as prizes.

- Summer Writing Camp: held annually in Ventura, California for young writers ages 8-18. Students have FUN while also learning how to improve central components of their writing, including dialogue, characterization, plot and setting, through various creativity-inducing writing exercises.

- Classroom Visits: Dallas regularly visits schools to speak about her career as a writer and the importance of reading and writing.

- Online Resources: visit www.writeonbooks.org for author interviews, book reviews, inspirational quotes, and more. Dallas also interacts with youth – and adults – through her blog http://dallaswoodburn.blogspot.com and her free monthly email newsletter. Subscribe at www.writeonbooks.org.

**Interested in joining Write On! For Literacy?**

We are always looking for new members who are passionate about reading and writing! Visit www.writeonbooks.org to learn more about what we do and share your ideas. You can also volunteer to host an event or start a chapter of Write On! in your town.

# About Dallas Woodburn

Dallas published her first book, a collection of short stories and poems titled *There's a Huge Pimple On My Nose*, when she was in fifth grade in 1998. A few months after publication it received a glowing review in the Los Angeles Times: "If you simply want to enjoy some remarkable writing, it would be hard to find a book more satisfying." *Pimple* has now sold more than 2,600 copies nationwide.

In 2005, Dallas worked with iUniverse to publish her second collection of stories, *3 a.m.*, which also garnered rave reviews and was featured on the nationally syndicated PBS book talk show "Between the Lines" hosted by the very talented and charismatic Barry Kibrick. Dallas's short fiction has been nominated for a Pushcart Prize and has appeared in numerous literary magazines including Monkeybicycle, Arcadia Journal, Cicada, flashquake, and The Newport Review, among others. She has also published more than seventy articles and essays in national publications including Family Circle,

Writer's Digest, Motherwords, The Los Angeles Times, and eight *Chicken Soup for the Soul* books. Since 2004, she has written the words and storyline of a monthly comic strip for the youth anti-drug magazine Listen.

Dallas has been interviewed on The Early Show on CBS and numerous radio programs. Her volunteer work has been recognized with a Jackie Kennedy Onassis/ Jefferson Award, a Congressional Award Gold Medal, and most recently a 2010 "Best of You" award from Glamour Magazine and Sally Hansen. In addition to her work with Write On!, Dallas has led workshops at the Santa Barbara Writers Conference and teaches a summer writing camp in her hometown of Ventura, California. She also serves as Youth Director on the board of the nonprofit organization SPAWN (Small Publishers, Artists and Writers Network).

In 2009, Dallas graduated *summa cum laude* from the University of Southern California with a B.A. in Creative Writing and a minor in Entrepreneurship. During her undergraduate years, she spent a semester studying abroad at the University of East Anglia in Norwich, England. This August, she is thrilled to be entering the renowned M.F.A. program in Fiction Writing at Purdue University.

When she's not at the keyboard, chalkboard or reading a good book, Dallas enjoys running, cooking, traveling, and spending time with loved ones.

Manufactured By:     RR Donnelley
                     Momence, IL  USA
                     February, 2011